A Manual of Snowmobiling

Also by the Author

High School Girls' Athletic Associations: Their
Organization and Administration

A MANUAL OF SNOWMOBILING

Judith A. Helmker

South Brunswick and New York:
A. S. Barnes and Company
London: Thomas Yoseloff Ltd

A. S. Barnes and Co., Inc.
Cranbury, New Jersey 08512

Thomas Yoseloff Ltd
108 New Bond Street
London W1Y OQX, England

ISBN 0-498-07794-2
Printed in the United States of America

This book is dedicated to
Lewis, Jon, Hollie
and Shellie,
and our snowmobile, Skeeter

Contents

Preface

There has been a dramatic change in the past three decades in the type of winter activities Americans find themselves participating in. A generation ago many people were hardly ever found out-of-doors during their leisure time, and most of them could be found in front of a roaring fire with a good book.

Not until the Industrial Revolution have wintertime sports become a part of the life of the average citizen. It has brought leisure for the masses and a breaking of the barriers of aristocracy. Accounts of primitive cultures indicate the importance of time given to winter activities directly related to the material prosperity of the people.

In 1932 the Olympic Games were held at Lake Placid, New York, and they caused a great deal of national interest in the out-of-door winter sports for people of all ages. As a result, the two leading sports that flourished were ice skating and skiing. Ice rinks were found in many parts of the community, sponsored by city, school, and private organizations. Many resort hotels added ice rinks to their recreational activities, which helped give rise to hockey and curling. Ice skating was even more popularized by the creation of artificial ice rinks. Skiing has grown so rapidly that today it stands as a multi-million-dollar commercial investment. There are numerous ski resorts that provide patrons with the most modern facilities and equipment.

Winter sports have been spurred on by the gigantic social revolution and affluent living. Not only do we have more free time from our occupations as a result of all these revolutions but our daily lives are less demanding physically. The housewife finds she can get her work done much faster, as can the farmer, the mechanic, and most every other worker. Early retirement and a longer life expectancy—characterized by better health and more vigor—all add to the new concepts of a sports-participating society. Income has been increased so that people have more money to spend on their recreational interests.

In a time of increased national tension and unrest—the youth rebellion, undeclared war, and problems of integration—a need for "family togetherness" is apparent. The need to reinforce the foundations of the American society is becoming quite evident. Family recreation provides parents and children with opportunities to play together, to recreate together, and to learn many things about one another.

The federal government has shown its awareness of these needs by instigating a number of programs that supplement recreation and provide people with an incentive to keep themselves mentally and physically fit. The government hopes that the gradual erosion that has been taking place will subside when people realize that what they do and how they do things affects them as well as the entire nation.

No one in America can deny the benefits from participating in recreational activities. As the population increases and the amount of free time increases, so does the need for new activities.

A new winter sport that has helped solve the problem of too much leisure time is snowmobiling, which only came about as a result of another need for people to be free to move around during the isolation of winter. The water, once limiting man's mobility, now provides many different outlets for recreation as well as industry. Hopefully, the snowmobile can tap these resources in the winter when the ground and water are frozen and covered with snow.

The snowmobile enthusiasts can engage in activities of snow cruising, racing, hunting, ice fishing, skijoring, just plain traveling, and many family and group activities—winter picnics, safaris, cook-outs, and camping—that were never dreamed possible.

The purpose of this book is to introduce you to the exciting world of snowmobiling and the benefits that can be derived from this new wintertime activity.

Judith A. Helmker

Acknowledgments

I would like to express my sincere appreciation to Dr. John Morovitz for his contribution on first aid.

Gratefully I wish to acknowledge the following manufacturers who graciously supplied me with information, statistics, pamphlets, photographs, and speeches: Arctic Enterprises, Bombardier Ltd, Evinrude Motors, Polaris, Ind., Rupp Manufacturing, Sno-Jet, and Yamaha Motor Co. Specific people from these companies are Robert Bromley, Arctic Cat; Marc Bourassa, Bombardier Ltd; Frank Ruth, Rupp; Wm. King of Health International.

I wish to express appreciation to all State and Federal Departments for the information on snowmobiling, and especially to Robert H. Myers and Roman Koenings, Department of the Interior, Lake Central Region; Jon Roethele, Michigan Department of Natural Resources; Robert Stevenson, Wyoming Recreation Commission; Curt Bernd, Minnesota Department of Conservation; Mary Vaughn, Washington Parks and Recreation Commission; Rolf Ertresvaag, North Dakota Park Service; and Gilbert A. Bliss, Massachusetts Department of Natural Resources.

I also wish to thank the United States Snowmobile Association, the International Snowmobile Industry Association, the Maine Snowmobile Association, and the Michigan Snowmobile Association.

I regret not being able to recognize certain people who have sent me information in spite of a diligent search as the result of many letters to trace sources for some original quotations.

Introduction
What's New—Snowmobiling

Today in our affluent living we find people suffering from a seasonal illness called "frigid leisuritis syndrome," or lots of time in the winter months with nothing to do. The miracle used to alleviate this dreaded illness is called "snowmobiling." A whole new decade has been launched, and what the future holds for this wonderful pastime is beyond your dreams or imagination. What other boon can equal this sport, which claims a 400-percent increase in participation in six years?

Once the ground is covered with the white powder of snow, the lakes turn solid, and the fragrance of the Northern White Pine lingers in the air, the dreaded illness starts to manifest itself. People complain of lassitude, emotional instability, irritability, chronic nagging, general aches and pains, and boredom; they develop an intolerable urge to lie around in front of the family television set. Physical activity diminishes and the body seems to suffer from an acute siege of physiological degeneration.

In years past the seasons were only distinguished by the temperature outside, the color of the ground, the number of leaves on the trees and their color, and the presence of certain animals. Man's work was the same no matter what environmental factors were present, and rare were the minutes spent in leisure time activities. Sunday, the traditional day of rest, meant quilting bees, family visits, and many hours of religious training.

Slowly this dreaded wintertime illness sets in. As the toll of casualties mounted, reaching a saturation point, the creation of snowmobiling came forth with hope for many thousands of sufferers. Winters are now never too long. "Frigid leisuritis" has been reduced, and the symptoms, known only to the northern winter residents, are slowly becoming nonexistent.

Snowmobiling is a dream come true and is available to anyone who feels the presence of the symptoms that cause you to become a wintertime drag. And so, as you stand there looking over the landscape, you know in your heart that today's snowmobiling is tomorrow's hope for wintertime happiness. And happiness is, of course, snowmobiling.

A Manual of Snowmobiling

1

The History

A cold gentle snowfall, a white-covered hill and valley—there is nothing more beautiful, or more exciting to winter sports enthusiasts.

Snowmobiling is instantly appealing to young and old, and the snowmobiler can go practically anywhere in this small car on skis. In a half hour you can travel farther into the wilderness than you could ever hike in a day. Most snowmobiles are easy to start and steer and have a host of safety features. From early November to late March, the snow-covered fields, lakes, forests, and plains become the silent domain of this new hardy sportsman. Snowmobiling unlocks many mysteries of hidden winter beauty and provides fun and excitement for all.

Everyone familiar with this winter sport knows its tremendous impact on the economy. Manufacturers report skyrocketing sales, increases in employment, and constant improvements on both machines and accessories. Not only has the industry itself boomed, but the small northern town that used to roll up its sidewalks when the temperature dropped below 40 degrees now has to prepare for its new breed of sports enthusiasts by stocking its restaurants, storing more gasoline and oil, and installing adequate heating facilities in its motels. Communities have set up clubs for the control of the sport and for arranging guided safaris for both hometown, inhabitants and visitors.

For a sport that has only been in existence since 1960, its history and heritage is shared by both the United States and Canada.

In 1928 in the northern Wisconsin woods, Carl Eliason, a man of many trades—and ailing from foot trouble—built a motorized toboggan. He attached a 2.5 horsepower gasoline outboard motor to the toboggan and added two wooden skis in the front. For four years he sold these machines (making improvements each year), and by 1932 his "snow flight," as he called it, used a converted motorcycle engine that hit speeds recorded over 40 mph. Two important principles were proved by the work of Eliason: first, a vehicle could be created to propel itself through snow, and second, the basic engineering was the most practical.

The first serious attempt to operate automotive equipment for a prolonged period of time came a few years after Carl Eliason's work. In 1933, when Admiral Richard Byrd led an expedition to the North Pole for meteorological and auroral work, he used two types of snow vehicles. The 10-20 Citroën was built in France during the first world war, and the 20-40 Cletrac was built by the Ford Motor Company in 1928. Although the Citroën and Cletrac were snow-traveling tractors they must be considered direct forerunners to the present two-passenger snowmobile and all-terrain vehicles. Ford saw no future for this snow-traveling tractor and discontinued production.

In 1922 in Wells, Nevada, Ab, Carl, and Herman Supp created a propeller-driven snow sled. This snow sled used a two-cylinder motorcycle engine and was powered by a French airplane engine. However, they did not put their creation into production.

In 1926, Joseph Armand Bombardier of Quebec built a wind sled that he hoped would someday prove to be an economical over-snow vehicle that would give more freedom to the people of Canada during the winter. He was further encouraged to free the winter snowbound Canadians when his child died of pneumonia because she could not be moved to medical facilities. Bombardier created his first snow vehicle, which used a Ford engine and large airplane propeller to drive it. Skis were used in front to steer the machine. A few years later the propeller was replaced by a single track. Mr. Bombardier also built an over-snow vehicle that resembled an army tank with skis in front. This vehicle held 30 passengers and was put into production in 1936, thus becoming the first commercial snowmobile.

In the late 1930s the Bombardier company, which primarily was concerned with building tractors, introduced a snowmobile that ran on rubber tracks driven by a sprocket. The body was built of plywood, and the motor was very large and heavy and pressed over the entire machine. With ground pressure very great, it was too difficult to steer and maneuver. A later model had a steel body and a rubber drive sprocket tandem suspension system that was similar to the Bombardier tractor.

In some northern towns in Canada and the United

States, the winter inhabitants often converted Model T Fords into a type of snowmobile by replacing the front wheels with skis and adding two wheels in back, which were connected by a metal chain drive belt. In 1926 at Three Lakes, Wisconsin, the first snow-vehicle race was held. These converted Model T's were used on a blocked-off, snow-covered street. Although they looked similar to the snowmobile of today, they cannot be considered in the same category because they were used only on hard-packed road surfaces and were steered by wheels.

During the latter part of World War II, the Bombardier snowmobile was used by the Allied Armed Forces in swampy areas in low countries. This machine had a double-width rubber track suspension system that was a major improvement since it reduced ground pressure and made the vehicle quite flexible.

In the late 1950s a lightweight gasoline engine was developed that enabled Joseph Bombardier and his son Germain to develop a more economical machine, which was called the "Ski Dog." It had a rubber-cleated tractor track with steel rods for added strength, and used the same principles of Eliason's machine of 30 years earlier. This original design kept the driver in back with the gas tank, engine, and skis ahead of him. The Ski Dog later became the Ski-Doo, and was the first two-passenger snowmobile to be built on a large scale for recreational and personal purposes. This machine weighed about 500 pounds and cost $1100. During the first years of production only 250 vehicles were produced. Today, more than 50 companies are putting out thousands of sleek and trim snowmobiles.

2

Ethics of Snowmobiling

The significance of a code of ethics for snowmobilers lies in an effort to control behavior by placing value on moral problems. It serves to guide and control participants in order to keep peace, to promote welfare, and to allow for the harmonious relationship between snowmobilers and non-snowmobilers. Without ethics, snowmobiling would probably perish.

Whenever a sport becomes organized, certain modes of conduct must be established and practiced until they become habits. Actions that are common to all group members must be approved and handed down through generations.

The ethics of snowmobiling can be easily understood if you keep in mind that there is one real purpose of the sport: enjoyment. Of primary concern is proper conduct in the use of the machine.

There are many ways of appraising and judging conduct. For instance, one snowmobiler must respect the

23

rights of others. Therefore we see that proper conduct must conform to our established ideals of right and wrong. Good conduct promotes happiness, which is a very important factor in the enjoyment we have established as the real purpose of snowmobiling.

Proper conduct is also based on wisdom and mature judgment. Judgment is based on conscience and a sense of duty that has been subjected to the experience of the individual. Wisdom also comes from experience, and unfortunately experience is often limited.

Good habits are important to the snowmobiler. Your response to certain situations is based on the habits you have developed, and the code of ethics should give people an idea of what the good ones are. If bad habits exist, the snowmobiler should be educated as to why they must be changed.

After good habits are in operation, two methods of enforcing them are public approval and taboos. Public approval of snowmobiling customs takes the form of praise of those who keep the rules and behave according to established standards. On the other hand, complaint, ridicule, and contempt are methods of enforcing compliance to the snowmobiling standards. Taboos do not enforce the rules as much as they help prohibit inappropriate conduct. They are important because they help form habits and operate through personal association among the snowmobilers under conditions that appeal to the emotions. Group opinion is another method of maintaining conformity.

The ethical rules of snowmobiling are aimed at providing a good relationship between the snowmobiler and everything he comes in contact with. His existence should provide for a full and harmonious working-together of all his abilities and attitudes. Although the code has an element of social approval it can only be considered a vehicle of moral judgment tending to develop etiquette.

Laws not only affect the code but impose restrictions that are in the best interest of the public. Snowmobiling is still young, and a rash of legislation has been passed by people who have had a too personal experience in the activity. Their sole reasoning is based on the complaints of those who feel their rights have been impinged. These people, many times, make their complaint without seeing the other side of the story. For example, the hunter poses legislation against snowmobiling because the noise frightens the animals and makes it impossible for him to stalk his game. He overlooks the fact that the snowmobiler has just as much right to spend his pastime in the woods as he does. Instead of forbidding the snowmobiler to use the woods, a mutual understanding should be worked out. But so far this has not been done fairly. What needs to be done is to have experienced snowmobilers assist in controlling the sport, as they are in a good position to understand the shortcomings. "Make haste slowly," an old adage, is the key to this particular problem. If snowmobiling had caught on slowly, adding only a few hundred participants each year, the problems could most likely be eliminated quite easily. But snowmobiling, by its very nature, is just too much fun, and once a person tries it he cannot help but join the sport.

The morals that are used to set standards for other sports and activities require people to estimate the value of their actions. Because snowmobiling is in its infancy, sometimes irrelevant petty complaints cause a great deal of excitement, which prevents the more important views from being considered. Major problems should be carefully examined and standards of conduct established, leaving these minor actions for a later time. A good example of this is the complaint of snowmobile noise. Instead of making regulations to limit this factor on the basis of its irritation to wildlife and man, use of acceptable, more distant pathways should be considered. Snowmobile manufacturers, aware of the noise problem, are working on its elimination, so why not concentrate on more important problems.

There are three general ways of improving snowmobiling conditions: the first and most basic is the control of the sport by those persons directly concerned; second is by organizing collective behavior; and third is coordinating mass education with intelligent direction. Snowmobilers must believe that the principles are universal, and are made in the best interest of the sport. The individual must understand that learning proper conduct prepares him to contribute to the growth of the sport.

Modern law emphasizes what man should (and should not) do. In creating a code of ethics, man's character must be considered, as it is this that gives reason to his actions. These rules, which are enforced by various agencies, require people to act in a way that meets general approval. There are some snowmobilers who tend to minimize the need to have a standard set of ethics. These people believe they already know what they should do based upon their knowledge of established law. They like to adhere to the tradition of individual freedom in interpreting the written law. Unfortunately, they do not stop to realize our present laws are inadequate, incomplete, and vague and apart from practical application of the sport.

It is only logical that we must look beyond the law to determine correct conduct, and even those who believe this code helps guide actions based on the law they must understand that it is not all-encompassing and can give no final answers. Codes do not only adhere to "the right," but they give people an idea of how to control impulsive action. Even if we set aside one code to be followed based on the golden rule, we still need a conception of what it actually means in terms of practice. The golden rule is a good basic rule, but it has two flaws. First, we can't be certain that well-being will be produced if others act exactly like we do. Second, many people treat themselves poorly and for others to conduct themselves similarly would be foolish. However, the code should start with the golden rule because of its universal validity.

The ethics created for snowmobiling should only limit action, and allow for individual discretion. Snowmobilers should be aware that their actions are not limited only to their small groups, but to all who participate in the sport, and that their decisions of right or wrong affect everyone.

It must be made clear to all that the future of snowmobiling relies entirely upon what is done in the beginning. Never before has a sport been swept into a community of such close intimate personal relations. No one can predict the future of this sport, but we can look at its present growth and predict a bright future. We can learn to face the problems of snowmobiling by creating a guide for conduct and obeying the laws that have been established. With our effort and support the sport will grow and flourish.

In 1969, a snowmobile code of ethics was proposed by a committee of representatives from the United States Forest Service, Bureau of Outdoor Recreation: Michigan Conservation Commission; Minnesota Conservation Department; Department of Lands and Forests, Ontario, Canada; United States National Park Service; and representative snowmobile manufacturers. For the time being this code is a good beginning.

Code of Ethics for Snowmobilers

1. I will be a good sportsman. I recognize that people judge all snowmobile owners by my actions. I will use my influence with other snowmobilers to promote sportsmanlike conduct.

2. I will not litter trails or camping areas. I will not pollute streams or lakes.

3. I will not damage living trees, shrubs, or other natural features.

4. I will respect other people's property and rights.

5. I will lend a helping hand when I see someone in distress.

6. I will make myself and my vehicle available to assist search and rescue parties.

7. I will not interfere with or harass hikers, skiers, snowshoers, ice fishermen, or other winter sportsmen. I will respect their right to enjoy our recreation facilities.

8. I will know and obey all federal, state, and local rules regulating the operation of snowmobiles in areas where I use my vehicle. I will inform public officials when using public lands.

9. I will not harass wildlife. I will avoid areas posted for the protection or feeding of wildlife.

10. I will stay on marked trails or marked roads open to snowmobiles. I will avoid cross-country travel unless specifically authorized.

3

Associated Activities

Fun is what snowmobiling—and cruising, camping, racing, hunting, ice fishing, skijoring, and snow-tobogganing—is all about. Sports that do not limit their activities grow in popularity.

When a snowmobile is first purchased its activities begin with snow cruising; later, when greater driving skill and courage are obtained, buzzing up and down hills is not enough. The many associated activities already mentioned add zest to the sport and provide greater winter fun, especially when combined with a picnic, a cookout, or even an overnight camping trip. Snow cruising is usually a brief excursion into the winter wilderness. There is an increased interest in night snow cruising and in both planned and unplanned safaris.

At first the use of the toboggan with the snowmobile became necessary when more people wanted to ride on the vehicle than there were seats or spaces. If a sleigh was not available, a toboggan was the next best method. Toboggans, inexpensive and easy to purchase, could also be used for hauling equipment. A stationary tongue should be fitted to avoid accidents as toboggans do not have any method of stopping themselves and may run into the back end of the snowmobile if a rope is used.

Skijoring is a sport in which the skier is drawn over the snow by a horse, which has been substituted by the snowmobile. The skill involved here is not to pile into the back end of the snowmobile after it has stopped or come to the bottom of a steep hill. The skier holds on to a rope with handles and travels about 20 to 30 feet behind the snowmobile. If more thrills are needed, the skier could add a parachute and try sky riding, in which he is launched behind snowmobiles going at least 20 miles per hour. Altitudes of 800 feet or more are reached on a 1000-foot nylon cord. When the sky rider wants to descend, the snow-mobiles slow down, decreasing the tension on the rope, which slowly and gently lowers the parachutist. It usually takes at least two snowmobiles to keep the parachutist aloft.

Hunting is allowed in some areas, but in most cases firearms are not allowed to be loaded while being carried on the snowmobile. Hunters may travel into the wilderness, but must not stalk game from the vehicle. The use of the snowmobile by hunters has lengthened the season for the average hunter and allowed him deeper penetration into wild areas. A problem does exist, however, with its noise. The greatest debate concerning snowmobiles is over their use during the various hunting seasons. Hunters who do not use them say the noise frightens game and interferes with the sport.

Fur trapping, especially in Canada, has found a tremendous use in the snowmobile. The trappers use it not only to set their traps but to carry in their kill. In the far north the snowmobile has all but replaced dog teams and made fur trapping a far more profitable business.

Like hunting, and trapping, the snowmobile has made it possible for the ice fisherman to visit lakes and streams never visited before. Because of the extreme cold associated with ice-fishing, automobiles and shanties were necessary, but they could only be used on lakes where ice depth could support the weight. In some regions, lakes would never completely freeze over until late December or even January, and then the heavy blanket of snow would make it impossible to get a car or shanty onto the lake. By using a snowmobile, the fisherman can get out to the lake for a morning or day of fishing, returning only to warm up or when the day's catch was reached.

In most states, and in Canada, the back roads that lead to most lakes are not plowed, so fishermen were required to travel long distances—by snowshoe if necessary—to reach their favorite fishing spot. The Conservation Department estimates that more than one million fishermen pursue the sport each winter in the United States, and that those who own snowmobiles spend more time fishing.

A question has been raised as to the effect of snowmobiles on the habits of fish. One report indicated that the snowmobile shadow did more to make fish scurry for cover than noise, but in any case no adverse results were obtained. Since boating does not seem to alter fish habits, the logic that snowmobiles will not harm them either is only common sense. Laws have been created that limit the distance snowmobiles can travel near ice fishermen. These laws are made for the snowmobiler as well as the fisherman. As with hunting, a conflict concerning noise also exists, as well as the problem of frozen slush made by snowmobiles.

If you plan on becoming a snowmobiling ice fisherman you will need the following equipment.

1. license
2. tackle
3. ice auger with guards
4. scoop
5. several spools of mono-filament 8010-pound test line
6. 3-foot stick or pole
7. bobber
8. tip-up
9. hooks
10. bait (minnows, dead smelt, herring chunks)
11. artificial bait
12. jigging rod

Snowmobiles have also assisted farmers and ranchers in getting their winter chores finished faster and with less effort. The farmer or rancher can use it to search for lost or stray animals, patrol fence lines, and carry equipment to fix fences and out buildings, saving him the work in the spring when there are many other jobs to be done.

Added to the list of associated activities are the uses of snowmobiles as all-terrain vehicles and all-season vehicles. These machines are not restricted to snow-covered areas but have been spurred on by the growth of snowmobiling. For work or play these vehicles have provided for people in all corners of the continent a means of transportation and recreation. The next few years will be important in the growth of this new industry. Believing there is going to be rapid progress, the Canadian All-Terrain Vehicle Manufacturers' Association was created to promote the industry, regulate sporting activities, and establish rules of competition in a unique all-year-round program. The first organized activity was a program held on Lake Simcoe in Barrie, Ontario, in February of 1970. The races included a slalom run, an obstacle course, several races, and games.

Snowmobile racing (Chapter 16) and camping (Chapter 12), which are also popular activities that have made the sport of snowmobiling more fun, are discussed later on at great lengths.

4

The Snowmobiler's Vocabulary

Each sport seems to have its own special jargon, snowmobiling included. Sometimes the sound of a sport, or the way it looks, is the basis for an associated name. For instance a "schush boomer" in skiing is a person who skis straight down the hill, usually out of control, increasing in speed every foot. The sound that is made is a long "schoooosh," and the person usually ends up at the bottom of the hill on his bottom.

When snowmobile enthusiasts get together, terms and phrases are used to denote special acts concerning the sport. It doesn't take long for a beginner to pick up these terms. Below is a list of frequently used snowmobile jargon.

ACT THE GOAT—Showing off a daring new maneuver.
BAIL OUT—Get off the snowmobile before it comes to a complete stop.
BEE OFF—Start rather suddenly on the snowmobile.

BLOWN ENGINE—A snowmobile engine whose cylinders have been converted and made larger than the factory-delivered ones.

BREAK OUT—Move away from the pack of snowmobilers during a race.

BURN THE TRAIL—Make a path through the wilderness with the snowmobile.

CHARGER—A person who tries hard to win a race but usually has difficulty coming in first.

CHEESE IT—Stop.

CLEAR OUT—Leave a camp or rest area.

COOL IT—Slow the snowmobile down and take your time.

CROSSED UP—Sideways sliding spin.

CROWD PLEASER—When the snowmobile leaves the snow and travels through the air with the driver standing.

CRY OFF—Eliminating yourself from a snowmobile race.

DITCHED—Running the snowmobile into an immovable situation.

DRAGGING YOUR FEET—Getting a distance away from a safari so they must wait until you catch up.

FIT OUT—Have the appropriate snowmobile clothing and equipment.

GET THE HANG OF IT—Learning by experience how to handle the machine.

GO EASY—Attempt to drive the snowmobile very carefully through a difficult trail.

GO THE WHOLE HOG—Get all the way up a steep hill without stopping.

GO TO SCHOOL—Learn how to drive better as a result of someone else's mistakes.

GUIDE—The person who leads the safari.

HANGING IT OUT—Leaning so the rear of the snowmobile sways out on a curve.

HANGING IT UP—An accident.

HOP IT—Make a fast start.

HOT LOT—Night racing snowmobilers.

HUNG OUT—Lost a race.

JUMP TO IT—Being quick about starting out on the trail.

KEEP TO—Follow the plan set up by the safari guide.

LAY ON—Pushing the snowmobile to go as fast as it can for an extended time.

LEANED—Thin out the fuel mixture.

LUNCHED—Burn the engine up.

MAKE THE GRADE—Reach the top of a difficult hill.

MEGAPHONE—Loud exhaust system.

MESS AROUND—Careless use of the snowmobile.

OUT OF THE HOLE—During a race the driver gets a fast start.

PEG OUT—Not finish the race.

POP IT—Allowing the snowmobile to leave the ground in front but keeping the tract in contact with the snow.

POWDER PUFF—Women's snowmobile race.

RACKED UP—An accident with the machine that rendered it inoperable.

RUN AWAY—One snowmobile in a race is a sure winner because the machine is farther from the pack.

SAFARI—When more than one snowmobile follows a planned trip.

SCRAMBLE AREAS—Designated areas where snowmobiles are allowed to operate.

SHOW OFF—A display of improper and unsafe behavior while on the machine.

TAKE ON—Challenge another to a race.

TAKE THE HILL—A challenge for a vehicle to climb a steep snow-covered hill.

TOUR SITE—Place where a trip into the wilderness will begin.

TRAILS—Paths made by the snowmobile track, or designated routes of travel.

TUNING THE EXHAUST—A new design to improve engine performance.

TURTLES—Slow snowmobiles in a race.

TWEAK THE CARBURETOR—Use a thin fuel mixture.

WARM UP—Preparing the machine for a trip or race by driving it slowly until the motor is warm.

WIPE OUT—Turning over a snowmobile.

5

The Industrial Effects
on the Economy

As adults our primary concern is creating comfortable living for ourselves and our children. Labor, if suited to the individual, is an enjoyable experience if it brings about the satisfaction of knowing you are contributing to the creative activities of your society. Since the industrial revolution and the coming of the machine age, civilization has not only changed its dwelling habits by clustering around industrial areas, but it has changed its economic structure to a point where masses have been liberated from long hours of toil and drudgery. As machines became more complex and were able to do more jobs, human labor was needed less. At first there was a problem of unemployment until society adjusted to the machine age. During this period of adjustment, economic life became quite complex, leaving many with the problem of how to use their leisure time.

We now consider leisure time activities not only recreational but desirable and beneficial to health and happiness. Today, because of the 40-hour work week and the monotony of many jobs, industry is seeking ways of filling the leisure time gap and its pockets at the same time.

Recreation is no longer considered a sin as it was in the days of our pioneer fathers. Because of the long hours and backbreaking work, their attitude toward recreation was poor. Now, no other civilization has ever had such an abundance of leisure time or such a healthy attitude toward it.

Leisure time can be blamed for both the creation of many blessings or the curse of many evils. Even though idleness is not frowned upon, it has caused a number of degenerative habits to be formed. This inappropriate behavior has become the forerunner to a number of other social problems. The leisure created by unemployment has caused many to become victims of mental disease. They become perplexed with many tortures of the mind that lead them to mischief making. Our society is becoming more aware of its responsibility for providing recreational facilities for all people. By keeping as many busy as possible, crime and delinquency decrease. Recreational activities prepare a person to face, with enthusiasm, his job and his social responsibilities.

Many people develop hobbies and seek desirable social activities to occupy their free time. But some take the opposite attitude and turn to alcohol, drugs, and other antisocial activities, that tend to destroy their social usefulness.

Snowmobiling as an industry, a recreational activity, and a sport has had an intensive impact on society. The primary interest as a commercial enterprise is of course money making, but the quality of recreation that this industry has offered is tremendous.

It is very unlikely that manufacturers of snowmobiles in the early 1960s ever knew the extent to which this machine would change the winter-time activities of people in all walks of life. According to Curt Bernd, Trails System Coordinator of the Minnesota Division of Parks and Recreation, "just about anyone and everyone participates in the activity. It has been stated that although 2% of the snowmobiles owned are used for racing, this 2% has contributed to about 90% of the popularity of the fast growing winter sport. Persons of all ages, descriptions, and backgrounds use snowmobiles on lakes, trails, road ditches, and family farms." In Minnesota alone, as of 1970, there are over 111,000 registered snowmobiles and over 15 manufacturers located within the state. Polaris Industries reports, "Ownership of snowmobiling runs approximately 39% rural, 39% suburban, and 22% in the metropolitan areas. About 70% of these owners also own a boat. In addition, 42% are campers and half of these owners take wintertime vacations. About 50% of these people have incomes in excess of $10,000. However, with the growing acceptability of the snowmobile, this income is changing quickly. In the snowbelt area, 25% of the male population have been snowmobiling last year (1968), nearly 40% have been snowmobiling at one time or another. Of this group, 7% now owns a snowmobile and there are 16% planning to buy in the near future."

Polaris, a leader in the snowmobiling industry, speculates a fantastic growth in the sport. In 1964, about 8,000 snowmobiles were manufactured and sold. In 1970 over half a million were produced and put into use.

Advertising has done a great deal to increase popularity and interest in snowmobiling. Magazines, newspapers, and television and radio coverage reach almost everyone, and manufacturers use all of these sources to get news of snowmobiling activities to the people. Snowmobiling and its associated industries, according to government figures, appear to be the fastest growing new industry in the United States and Canada. Beyond the manufacturing of machines comes an increase in parts production, engine and rubber production, and an increased work capacity in areas of engineering, industrial design, tool and die making, office personnel, accounting, and administration. Add this to all the fringe activities concerned with the production of accessories and the influence of these machines on cities, towns, and resort areas, and you can soon visualize the multi-million dollar investment.

In 1970 the snowmobiling industry grossed over 300 million. Arctic Industries, in their annual stockholders report, indicated their net sales in 1968 were $8,181,736, while their 1969 sales rose to $21,755,765. This indicates a 266 percent increase in just one year. Stockholders in this corporation increased their earning from 41 cents in 1968 to $1.24 in 1969, and were further aided by a 4 for 1 stock split. The industry's growth has forced manufacturers to step up production as well as increase the number of dealer-distributors. In 1970 over 10,000 dealers sold over 200 makes of almost 50 brands of snowmobiles. Sales have exceeded expectations. According to the International Snowmobile Industry Association, 285,000 vehicles were produced between March 1969 and March 1970. While only 80,000 Units were built in 1965, the expected production in 1971 is estimated to be over 350,000.

The snowmobile industry cannot ignore the importance

that racing has had on its sales. Racing gives extensive public exposure and acts as a research arena to test new concepts. Knowledge is gained as to the value certain new designs have on the safe and efficient operation of the machine, which in turn is passed on to the 98 percent population of recreation snowmobilers.

There is little doubt that the direct impact of snowmobiling on the economy, as well as on the direct relationship of people and their lives, will continue to influence wintertime habits. The sport has become so popular that state and national government agencies have established trails in state and national parks and forests. In 1969 Minnesota had 23 marked trails and is attempting to create an interstate trail between Wisconsin, Michigan, and North Dakota.

In 1970 the world's largest producer of snowmobiles was the Bombardier Ltd. of Valcourt, Quebec, with over 100,000 vehicles manufactured during the season. Second is Polaris Industries of Roseau, Minnesota. Third is Arctic Enterprises Inc. of Thief River Falls, Minnesota, and fourth is Outboard Marine Corp Ltd., Peterborough, Ontario. These four companies account for an estimated 75 percent of all snowmobile sales. Most of the 50 manufacturers create special vehicles for special occasions (racing, water travel, mini-minded people, and regular recreation). Prices of these vehicles range from $400 to over $1300, the greater expense being in those machines with more power, speed, and rider comfort.

6

The Law

The responsibility of city, state, and national lawmaking bodies concerning the use of snowmobiles has been delegated appropriately according to constitutional privileges. Everyday an increased amount of news concerning snowmobiling laws and regulations makes headlines.

Lawmakers are constantly being told of the irresponsible minority of snowmobile owners who jeopardize the rights of other snowmobilers by breaking established rules and regulations. Laws are made to protect all people and their rights, and when someone breaks a law, this reflects on those directly involved in the total activity. Most snowmobilers are careful and courteous, but there are a few irresponsible ones that must be restrained and for whom these laws are set up.

Law enforcement agencies and non-owners beg for more stringent regulations. Even people who simply read about problems that snowmobilers have caused feel they must help prevent this group from hurting themselves or others.

Because they are directly concerned, snowmobilers must have a chance to help set up new laws.

There is no doubt that snowmobiling is a controversial subject. Any new idea that has increased so rapidly is bound to make a tremendous impression. After any new activity begins, only experience can shape its shortcomings. This is the reason why some ordinances are too hasty. In many states, a rash of regulations have been put into effect by people with little personal knowledge of the sport. Hundreds of ordinances in communities of both the United States and Canada have produced confusion because of the haste in which they were created. Much dissent is justified, some is not. In some areas, the only rules or laws are those of the "public nuisance" variety, which were established generations ago and have become archaic in time. Other areas have pushed legislation and not taken time to foresee the problems of enforcement. Many law enforcement agencies are not equipped to cope with the transgressors or determine when public rights have been infringed upon because the legislation is confusing, complicated, unrealistic, too restrictive, and in some cases very contradictory.

Some states and some provinces of Canada have concentrated their efforts in finding out how legislation affects the sport; they don't just listen to the cries of those who say snowmobilers are a menace to man and wildlife. Ronald Speers, conservation chief in Maine, came to the defense of snowmobiling in a television speech by saying, "I recognize that there is a segment of our people who look upon the snow machine as an enemy of the 'forever wild' concept. Until such time as those same advocates can show me that the summer user is not as much of a culprit as the winter recreationalist, I must remain objec-

tive in my thinking." Some feel the state of Maine has
done a good job in establishing fair legislation and many
have used its 1969 snowmobiling law as a model. Basically
all states require snowmobiles to be registered, and forbid
their travel on public highways. Maine feels that snowmobiling has more positive effects on society than negative
ones and cites no judicial case ever appearing in courts
where a conviction of law breakage was proven. Now this
does not mean that wrongs have not been committed; it
means only that transgressors have not been apprehended
and brought to justice.

Most states feel that snowmobiling does not violate the
ideal of natural park settings, and they have established,
within the limits of both state and national parks, thousands of trails and scramble areas.

Acadia National Park conducted a survey in 1968 concerning the impact of snowmobiling, which included
equipping deer with radio transmitters that monitored
their vital signs. The study showed that the animals had no
adverse reactions when snowmobiles approached.

The conservation department receives complaints concerning the destruction of plants and trees. However,
studies show that this damage can be avoided by simply
closing certain areas where it might occur. Conservation
officers have been called upon to enforce some of the new
legislation concerning snowmobiling as well as the
presently established laws of conservation. The general
consensus is that they find most snowmobilers to be law-
abiding citizens and encourage their activities in the
wilderness. However, they have set objectives to find,
arrest, and prosecute violators as well as to educate snowmobilers in safe and sane driving habits that will create
a favorable relationship. The knowledge from past expe-

rience shows that snowmobilers and nonsnowmobilers must get along, knowing and understanding that there is enough beauty and natural resources available to all if only they will both respect the rights of everyone. The only thing that is asked by the conservation department is that the wilderness remain undisturbed. Interpretation is by common sense as well as the established law.

Another problem in need of legislation is at what age should a person be allowed to drive a snowmobile. More and more accidents occur each year with children driving snowmobiles unsupervised by adults. Also, many of the reports of animal harassment and wildlife destruction have been blamed on the actions of unthinking youths.

In Minnesota, the Department of Conservation passed a law requiring all children from 14 to 17 to take a safety training program. The classes are based on a series of studies and tests, and after the students finish the course they become eligible to cross public roads. This is just the beginning of the public's awareness that through education snowmobiling will become a safe sport. The question still remains as to what age is a person responsible enough to handle all the problems that arise during participation of the sport. Bill Severson, Snowmobile and Firearms Safety Coordinator for the Minnesota Department of Conservation, states: "This age factor has become a vitally important one. A lot depends on the child, his parents, conditions of the terrain and other situations. If we're talking for example about cutting back on the throttle and looking at some wide open spaces, some young people under 14 can safely handle the snowmobile. Unfortunately though, people, young and old alike, are simply not using good judgment. They have a large investment here and apparently are not too concerned about protecting it. . . .

Parents who impose no restrictions on their children—the ones who let them come and go as they please and have no guidelines to follow—are the ones most likely to care less how their children conduct themselves on a snowmobile."[1]

At one time parents had to use their better judgment in allowing children under 14 to drive the snowmobile on public land where someone else may get hurt. However, now new legislation forbids the use of snowmobiling by persons under 14 years of age.

It is quite obvious that legislation is necessary to control the sport, but it is also obvious that this legislation should be based on fact, not hearsay. Snowmobile legislation and any restrictions imposed must be as fair to the snowmobiler as it is to the general public.

Michael R. Hoffman,[2] publisher of *Sno-Mobile Times*, lists five factors that must be considered in snowmobile legislation.

1. Time and experience will sooner or later guide the officials to set controls which will satisfy both the snowmobiler and non-snowmobiler.
2. Snowmobile clubs have already done much (and will no doubt do lots more) to aid legislators and government officials to stipulate the kind of rules and regulations which do not deprive the snowmobiler of the full enjoyment of his sport, yet give ample protection for the general public. Many have established safety programs and are educating both their members and non-members in law-abiding snowmobiling.
3. Many governmental and quasi-public bodies have quickly appraised the vicissitudes of the new winter

1 Jerry Hoffman, "At What Age Snowmobiling," *Sno-Mobile Times*, February 1970, p. 69.
2 Hoffman, Michael R., "Snowmobile Ordinances—Too Hasty," *Sno-Mobile Times*, February 1970, p. 1.

recreation and, realizing that the sport is here to stay, are properly propagandizing to help the snowmobile enthusiast to use his vehicle with safety for himself and others.

4. The snowmobile industry is working rapidly to provide more inherent safety features in their machines and are lending a helping hand wherever and to whomever it can to advise and instruct in the careful handling of snowmobiles.

5. Newspapers, magazines and other media are intensely and widely publicizing snowmobiling telling all sides of the story—both good and bad—which is a healthy sign that the snowmobiler and the general public can become fully knowledgeable in order to eventually settle on mutually satisfactory terms for the continuing growth of the sport without undue deprivation for either.

In a recent study by this author of the various laws in each state and two provinces of Canada, the following regulations seem to be characteristic. It must be realized that not all these laws are in effect in all states, nor with the same amount of emphasis and enforcement.

1. All snowmobiles must be registered.

2. All snowmobiles must carry their registration numbers where they can be easily seen.

3. Snowmobiles that are operated on private land of the owner are exempt from registration.

4. Dealers must secure a dealer's license.

5. No one can operate the vehicle on controlled access highways or on their right-of-ways.

6. Registered snowmobiles may cross public roads, but not controlled access highways.

7. Snowmobiles must yield the right-of-way to all highway vehicles while attempting to cross roads.

8. Snowmobiles may be operated on unplowed roads that are used by conventional motor vehicles.

9. Snowmobiles may not cross roads from sunset to sunrise on main traveled roads.

10. Under no circumstances shall snowmobiles be driven on main traveled roads or their right-of-way unless there has been an emergency declared.

11. It is against the law to drive recklessly (each state deals with this differently).

12. It is against the law to drive under the influence of liquor (each state sets its limits differently).

13. It is against the law to endanger the life of anyone with the snowmobile.

14. Speed has not been regulated, but most states insist it should be within reason for existing conditions.

15. No one under 14 may cross a public road.

16. No operator's license is required—yet.

17. All snowmobiles must have a muffler.

18. All persons must obtain permission to drive their snowmobile on property that is not their own.

19. When you are on someone else's property, he has the right to stop you and ask for identification.

20. Snowmobiles used just for racing do not have to be registered or have mufflers or lights if they are used only in racing areas.

21. You may not operate the snowmobile on railroad tracks.

22. During emergencies, snowmobiles are used under the jurisdiction of the local police agency.

23. Snowmobiles must have a front light and a taillight, both which must be on before dusk and be able to be seen at a distance of at least 500 feet.

24. Non-resident snowmobiles are usually welcomed in each state without registration.

25. When an accident occurs where damage is over $100 it must be reported to a police agency.

26. Law enforcers are state police or similar organizations, conservation officials, forestry officers, and local police.

27. Penalty for violations range from $10 to $100 for each offense, and in most cases the snowmobile license is not taken away.

28. Anyone driving the vehicle is responsible for his own actions whether he is the owner or not.

29. There is a $10 to $100 fine for littering.

30. In State Parks all the above rules are in effect as well as the following:

a. Vehicles must stay on designated trails.

b. Vehicles must not be driven when there is insufficient snow.

c. Racing is usually not allowed.

d. Some parks require permits for snow travel.

31. Snowmobilers may not carry loaded firearms.

32. It is against most laws to harass wildlife.

33. Snowmobiles may not be driven on freeways.

One last problem of legislation concerns the access of machines across the border between the United States and Canada. Many operators unknowingly have violated international law by traveling back and forth across the border.

United States citizens may not travel at will to Canada and back even in sparsely populated areas, as the laws of Immigration and Naturalization require that all persons report to a customs officer. The law states that any vehicle coming into the United States must report his presence at the nearest port of entry. Because of an increase in violations, a border guard is in the process of being created. The penalty for violating these laws is up to $100 for every offense. If merchandise is brought into Canada it is subject to seizure and additional fine. Passengers are also fined and the driver assessed an additional $500 for each rider. Since relations between the United States and Canada are favorable at this time it is only common sense to abide by all legislation.

Another point that must be considered is the use of snowmobiles in connection with felonious acts. In some areas the winter crime rate has soared, and summer homes, once safe from thieves and vandals because of inaccessibility, are becoming the objects of felonies. Even in rural communities, snowmobiles have been used for robberies and other acts of violence. However, with all the shortcomings of snowmobiling, there are also evidences of the good for which they have been used. The future of snowmobiling lies in how effectively the sport is controlled so that its values will virtually offset its inadequacies.

7

Legal Liability
and Insurance

Any recreational activity carries with it responsibilities for
the well-being of all participants. If the activity is well
managed and supervised, problems of liability will be
minimal. In snowmobiling it is important that safe prac-
tices preclude all other matters, because in all instances
the driver is liable. Having enough insurance could make
the difference between financial tragedy and a successful
outcome to an unpleasant situation.

No matter what safety factors are taken into consideration and followed, accidents still happen. Knowing how
and where problems might occur, and taking steps to
alleviate them before something serious happens, is important.

Generally, the snowmobile driver is liable for damages
he causes as result of negligence where there are personal

injuries or property damage. However, the key word here is negligence, and proving this in a court of law is sometimes very difficult. The heartache and inconvenience caused by a negligence suit can be avoided if the driver will act with good common sense at all times.

Another liability the snowmobiler must be aware of is that of trespassing. The landowner may not willfully injure a trespasser and must by law place warnings of such dangers as vicious animals, pits, and holes. If a landowner has given permission to the snowmobiler to ride on his property he is responsible for the safety of this individual within reason. This is the main reason why property owners do not allow snowmobilers on their property; they do not want to be liable.

In most states landowners who allow snowmobilers to travel on their property must provide "ordinary and reasonable" care. This aspect of liability is subject to interpretation by the courts of various states.

Insurance for most snowmobile owners protects them from damage caused by themselves or others. Up until 1968, snowmobiles were covered in most states by homeowners insurance. However, many companies have excluded this coverage because of its use on public land. If a snowmobile is in storage on your property it is in many cases covered against such things as theft, fire, and vandalism. Each homeowner should check his individual policy to see if this coverage is available. If your home was purchased since 1968, your homeowners policy most likely does not cover the snowmobile.

Snowmobiles should have an insurance policy that covers theft, collision, sinkage, public liability, public damage, and personal injury. Make sure it covers any driver—not just the owner—and the vehicle from damage caused by another. Towing is another feature that should be checked into.

Most insurance policies are considered liability and physical damage policies, but some may be written to include an all-risk clause. Most policies cover the trailer used to transport the snowmobile.

Insurance, although rising annually, costs from $10 to $50 per year. Some companies are leaning toward group policies and have special rates for clubs. The United States Snowmobile Association has had an insurance program through the Hallmark Insurance Company of Madison, Wisconsin. The Michigan International Snowmobile Association has membership coverage with a disability income, which comes free to members. Competitive drivers may also purchase this insurance through the association for about $15 per year. Costs of club insurance policies do change from year to year as their membership gets greater, accidents more frequent, repairs more costly, and coverage more comprehensive.

Because snowmobiling is such a new sport, insurance companies find it difficult to predict the amount of loss and administration cost of the insurance programs. Sometimes the policyholder may find his rates suddenly higher because of a poor prediction the year before. Companies also have difficulty in determining the type of coverage for the type of vehicle to be insured. Most snowmobiles are designed to travel over snow and ice, but some are geared for any terrain and must have extra coverage. A list of companies that offer snowmobile insurance can be found in the Appendix.

8

The Machine

The first requirement of snowmobiling is to know your machine. When the snowmobile is purchased there is a manual that explains how it works and how to care for it. It is very important to become completely familiar with the working parts and controls, and with how the snowmobile responds. The manual also gives information that you should know in order to obtain peak performance and pleasure in operation.

Even though snowmobiles differ in looks, they are all basically constructed alike. The standard components are a 2-cycle engine, chassis, track drive system with suspension, and power converter system.

The chassis is the frame of the machine on which the other parts are mounted. In front a pair of skis steer the snowmobile by a handlebar carrying a throttle and brake control. Behind the handlebars is a bench seat, and below is a revolving drive belt. Here is a simple drawing of a basic snowmobile showing parts with which the owner should become familiar.

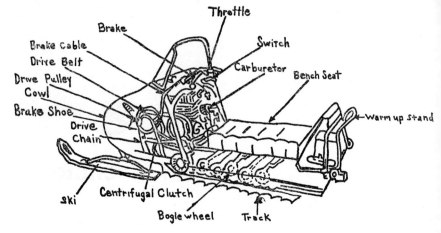

Throttle
Brake
Brake cable
Drive Belt
Drive Pulley
Cowl
Brake Shoe
Drive Chain
Ski
Switch
Carburetor
Bench Seat
Warm up stand
Centrifugal Clutch
Bogie wheel
Track

(Courtesy The Extension Service, University of Vermont)

Most snowmobiles were produced to give years of dependable service, and most manufacturers guarantee their machine for a certain period of time, as long as the owner does not attempt to make repairs himself. Manufacturers warn owners that these vehicles were not designed or equipped for highway use.

When purchasing a snowmobile for the first time there are certain things to take into consideration. First, don't be confused by the price, as most snowmobiles range from $600 to $1600. Buying the most expensive machine does not necessarily mean you have purchased the best, even though a higher priced snowmobile offers a long range savings because it is usually built better. Basically you are paying for top performance, less upkeep, and the extra conveniences. Second, the size of the machine you purchase is influenced by the type of driving it will be subject to. A small one with a lot of speed may be fine for a single man, but a larger one with more pulling power is better for the family man. Third is the speed factor. Most machines have sufficient horsepower to drive the snowmobile easily through most winter terrains. The faster the machine goes the more dangerous it becomes. In selecting which snowmobile would be best also consider styling, stability, versatility, and trail performance. Also choose a machine you can depend on, as you surely would not like it to give out when you're far from home.

After the purchase has been made, get acquainted. As a good snowmobiler become familiar with the machine's weight, engine size and horsepower, track qualities and performance, fueling, and correct maintenance.

Maintaining the snowmobile can be made easier by following some recommended rules.

Special Precautions

1. When starting a snowmobile in below-zero weather, the machine should be tilted on its side or lifted onto its warm-up stand, and the engine revved to warm up the track.

2. If the machine has not been used in sub-zero temperature, the rubber track becomes stiff. The driver should give the rubber a chance to limber up or he may burn the side of the drive belt where it touches the engine pulley.

3. If the snow forms ice crystals inside the track, it may become so hard that the track stops turning. If this happens turn the machine on its side or onto its warm-up track and run the engine.

4. If the machine has been wet it will need a complete lubrication of working parts. Water weakens the ability of grease to lubricate, especially in very cold temperatures.

5. Machines should be greased every 15 to 18 hours or more if they are unusually wet.

6. If the throttle cable fails it may be operated by hand if it is exposed. If it is hidden behind a panel, the panel must be removed.

7. If the machine gives a retching effect, adjust the motor drive belt tension.

On the Trail Problems

1. Vapor-lock may be taken care of by first giving the machine a chance to rest so that the fuel has a chance to cool down. If the muffler area is packed with snow, further vapor locks will be eliminated and the machine will keep running.

2. Most machines come equipped with a notched pulley behind the starter. If the starter rope breaks, the rope can be knotted and wrapped around the pulley.

3. If you lose your starter key, sometimes another snowmobile key will work. If not, the driver can cut the ground wire between the switch and the engine and start the engine with the choke.

4. If a ski breaks on the trail, the rider may drive the machine by leaning to the good ski side.

5. If the snowmobile has to be hauled from a trail, another machine may haul it by tieing the skis together. It will help if the drive belt is disconnected. If the distance is great, skis should be reversed and the rear of the machine lifted onto the snowmobile that is doing the hauling.

Carburetor Problems

Dirt may cause the snowmobile to stop because it has filtered beneath the needle and seat assembly and clogged the check-valve seal that is used to keep fuel in the line that leads to the carburetor. The machine may be started by two people. One person blows into the fuel tank to create pressure and the other cranks the engine until the fuel is drawn into the carburetor. The machine will usually keep running but it will need further attention.

Mixing Fuel

1. Use a good grade gasoline and a separate, clean container to mix the gas and oil.
2. Use a fresh mixture of gas and oil.
3. Use a clean funnel with a fine screen to pour the mixture into the gas tank.
4. Do not mix gas and oil in temperatures below 32 degrees.
5. Be sure the gas can does not have water in it as it may cause the gasoline to freeze or improper spark plug firing.

Throttle Lever

Be sure the throttle cable is working before starting the engine or it may stick, sending the snowmobile in motion when the engine is started.

Drive Clutch System

1. Lubricate the two clutches often as directed by your snowmobile manual. Too much grease in the wrong place may also cause poor operation.
2. Check the amount of pressure applied by the belt between the clutches. If the machine has a grease gun fitting, these clutches need only a small amount of lubrication.

3. Adjust the drive chain and replace it when necessary. This chain receives a great deal of pressure and improper tension will result in undue wear of the track and other drive components. If tension is not equal the snowmobile will veer to one side.

4. Check and grease bogie wheels and springs often. A broken spring may cause damage to the track.

Track

Check the track of the snowmobile to see if it is properly aligned and that the clearance on each side in the rear is the same. Check the manual for methods of proper adjustment.

Battery

The battery is an often abused part of the mechanical operation and should be checked frequently to be assured of top performance. Battery acid may damage more than the battery, so check to see if the caps are on tight.

Transmission Belt

The belt will wear with use and needs to be checked often. Even if the belt does not show a great deal of wear you wouldn't want to be miles from home when it snaps. After a reasonable amount of time, buy a new belt, install it, and keep the used one as a spare.

Brakes

Check and tighten the brakes frequently. If hand brakes do not have enough flexibility they may not stop the snowmobile properly. Never drive a snowmobile if the brakes are not operating correctly.

Skis

Skis must be parallel. Check this by measuring both the front and back distance.

Spark Plugs

If the engine seems sluggish check the spark plugs, and be sure to use the correct plug size if you desire efficient operation. Keep a spare plug on hand for emergencies. You may clean the spark plugs by scraping the caked carbon away with a wire brush.

Slide Track Suspension

The slide track may be replaced by a split-rail slide assembly, which is designed to bolt onto the bogie wheel mounts. This provides for a smoother ride and better control at high speeds.

Storing the Snowmobile

1. Store the snowmobile off the track and skis, drain and clean the fuel tank, clean the carburetor and screen. Run the engine to avoid the remaining gas from causing rust, loosen the track tension, remove the drive belt, oil the skis and keep them in a dry, well-ventilated place.
2. Before using next winter, remember to adjust the track tension, lubricate moving parts, paint (if necessary), replace the drive belt, and add the fuel mixture.

General Considerations

1. Always allow the engine to warm up before putting the machine in gear.
2. Start slowly, avoiding sudden starts and stops.
3. If the machine has a warm-up stand, use it.
4. If the machine needs attention because it is not op-

erating properly, never make repairs while the engine is running. Also it is wise to disconnect spark plug wires when checking the engine or drive unit.

5. If the engine is cold, adjust the choke. If there is difficulty in starting, the carburetor must be primed.

Driving Tips

1. Sit so the upper part of the body can sway with the machine, and sit back with your weight on the track. Snowmobiles are difficult to steer if there is weight on the skis. Take a firm grip on the handlebars so you won't lose control.

2. Lean into turns. When making a curve, lean to the opposite direction.

3. Kneeling while riding offers a high degree of balance but is a little more dangerous.

4. When you approach a steep hill, speed must be increased or the machine may bog down in the snow or slide back down the hill because it has insufficient power to reach the top. Open the throttle while going up and as soon as you hit the crest, let up on it. You must keep your knees flexed to take the shock when the skis hit the ground.

5. Riding downhill may be exhilarating but it is easy to lose control if you are not careful. It is safer to come downhill in a zigzag in order to avoid too much speed. Always drive in control.

6. While on a wooded trail stay in the center of the path so you are not clipped by low trees. Avoid riding on the down wind side of trees as snow cavities are frequently found here and may tip the machine over or cause it to get stuck.

7. If you do not have a reverse and are stuck, stand on

the right side and lift the machine while you feed it a little gas with your right hand. Only accelerate it enough to move the machine to the top of the snow; too much gas will make the track dig deeper into its hole.

8. Even though most snowmobiles are built for two, the extra rider adds extra weight making the skis harder to control. The second rider should lean with the driver, hold firmly to the side bars and be as relaxed as possible.

Further information on Driving Tips can be found in the chapter on Safety.

One last consideration. As was mentioned before, most snowmobiles are basically the same. Below is a list of the various snowmobile parts and some of the problems that might be associated with them.

Part	Function	Problem
Throttle	accelerating the snowmobile	cable may cause throttle to stick
Light switch	turns head and tail lights on and off	
Primer	starts a cold engine	
Choke	forces gas into the carburetor	
Electric start	special feature that uses battery power to start the machine	weak battery may keep engine from starting
Fuel gauge	shows amount of fuel in the tank	icing may give an incorrect reading
Battery	electrical power for electric models	may keep engine from starting
Bogie system	wheels used to turn track	wear may cause damage to track

Track	provides power for movement	breakage will render vehicle immovable
Frame	attachment for all moving parts	
Tank cap	cover for gas tank	loss could be dangerous
Taillight	light in rear	breakage could mean a rear collision
Bench Seat	rider comfort	
Drivebelt	connector between pulleys to provide driving power	breakage will render vehicle immovable
Reverse Control	allows machine to back up	
Pulley Guard	protects against belt breakage	
Headlight	light in front	breakage could mean a front-end collision
Springs	absorb shock and provide rider comfort	
Brake	stops snowmobile	loss could cause a serious accident
Handlebars	steering device where throttle and brake are located	
Cowl	front of snowmobile that protects engine and working parts	
Windshield	plastic protector for driver from movement elements	

9

Preparation for the Trip

There are numerous places open to snowmobiles: state and national parks, lake and privately owned property, golf courses, ski resort areas, and private resorts. A most pleasurable experience, however, is using the snowmobile on land that is your own. Summer cottage owners have begun to open their doors in the winter, and many people are converting summer-only cottages into all-year around ones. To find out what public and private facilities are available write to your state conservation department, tourist council, or the Federal Forestry Department in Washington. A list of other addresses is found in the Appendix.

Although ski areas generally do not like to mix skiers and snowmobiles, they are opening special trails for the sole purpose of snowmobiling. Golf clubs in the far northern areas where snow is deep have found a new use for their facilities. However, clubs in areas where snow is not deep for many weeks out of the winter hesitate to allow snowmobiles because of possible damage to greens.

Wherever you go, whether for a day or week of snow-mobiling, the outing requires a few before-hand preparations.

It is a wise idea to definitely lay out a route and set up a tentative schedule of events. The only time this isn't necessary is when you are planning a short trip in the area of a cottage. Basically, the things that should be done before setting out are:

Determine and list needed equipment.

Create an itinerary in duplicate.

Only set out on the trip if you are physically and mentally prepared.

Know your area or have someone in your group who does.

Never go long distances alone.

Always leave a copy of the itinerary.

Plan your time and distance carefully. Don't under-estimate the time your trip will take; 30 mph is a difficult pace to maintain so it is better to plan on 15 mph. Do not plan to cross land that is privately owned unless you have obtained permission beforehand.

Plan for re-fueling.

Check the condition of any frozen lakes that you must travel on by contacting the nearest police agency.

Have a basic tool kit that also includes first aid and survival supplies.

If you are to be out after dark be sure to have an extra headlight and taillight.

Know your trail markers.

Know the snow—is it dry, or wet—and check into the weather forecast.

Heath Recreational Sales Division in Richmond, Michigan, suggest 20 ideas to follow for planning a safari.

1. A safari should consist of no more than 30 snowmobiles. (You may want to consider more, and in that case there should be an experienced snowmobiler for every ten machines.)

    a. All snowmobiles shall be checked to make sure they are mechanically sound.

    b. All gas tanks shall be full.

    c. Each machine shall carry its own type extra plug and drive belt.

2. Never let anyone leave the safari and go off alone. (First rule of safety—never snowmobile alone.)

3. Each driver shall keep at least three machine lengths apart.

4. A novice snowmobiler should be required to read the snowmobile booklet on safe snowmobiling prepared by Bombardier Ltd. and the National Safety Council.

5. A novice should also have a few minutes of instruction, practice, and familiarization before leaving on a safari.

6. The time limit of the safari should be up to the judgment and experience of the guide or leader. It could be from two hours to all day. (Always try to return before dark. Only experienced snowmobilers should drive at night who are familiar with the trail and terrain.) Arrange trail with half-way point for anyone wishing to return to lodge or camp sooner.

7. The proper clothing and accessories should be worn at all times. Beware of frostbite. If the temperature is 15 degrees and you are traveling 20 mph, the equivalent temperature is 19 below zero; at 40 mph, it's 30 below (see the windchill chart). Anyone riding in a sled will become colder much sooner and should be dressed warmer than the driver.

8. Heavy, snow-resistant, water-repellent pants and jack-

ets (or snowmobile jump-type suits), felt pack-type shoes and rubbers (or snowmobile boots), heavy gloves or mittens, face mask or safety helmet, goggles, and, on long safaris, spare mittens, socks, and scarves are recommended. Special care should be taken not to wear anything tight.

9. There should be clearly marked trail signs, and if you plan to go off into the backwoods and trail blaze, you must have an experienced guide familiar with the area. If a road is to be crossed, flag men should be sent ahead to warn traffic.

10. All children under ten years of age should be accompanied by an adult.

11. A first-aid kit and some one experienced in emergency first-aid should accompany each safari, no matter how small or large the group or time limit of the trip.

12. On long safaris a mechanic may accompany the group and carry extra parts, tools, and gas. This person should always follow at the rear of the safari.

13. If a machine has broken down and cannot be repaired in the field, have an experienced person tow it back to the lodge or repair station. (A machine can be towed on an aluminum sheet that can be rolled up.)

14. Leave early in the morning after a good night's rest, to enjoy the best of the day. Make frequent stops for rest and refreshments, and on long safaris plan a lunch or cook-out, camp style, at a scenic spot. (Send scouts ahead to set up a warm-up station.)

15. Draw out a rough map of where you will be going and how you will be returning. Explain distance and terrain to all drivers.

16. There should always be a leader and a drag rider, who are familiar with the trail, and ice conditions (if

you plan to cross a river or lake) , and they should always be alert to changing weather conditions. The leader and drag man should be identified to everyone.

17. If the safari will take you over rough terrain, be sure everyone can negotiate the trail without injury.

18. Each driver should be constantly aware of the machine behind him.

19. Special care should be taken when driving through tree plantations or private land (you must have permission) , or crossing at gates and fences.

20. Good judgment and safety measures should be adhered to at all times, observing the regulations of the state snowmobile laws. Never let anyone become reckless. A safe safari is a fun safari.

WIND CHILL CHART

Estimated wind speed in MPH	actual thermometer reading (°F.)									
	50	40	30	20	10	0	−10	−20	−30	−40
	Equivalent temperature (F)									
Calm	50	40	30	20	10	0	−10	−20	−30	−40
5	48	37	27	16	6	−5	−15	−26	−36	−47
10	40	28	16	4	−9	−21	−33	−46	−58	−70
15	36	22	9	−5	−18	−36	−45	−58	−72	−85
20	32	18	4	−10	−25	−39	−53	−67	−82	−96
25	30	16	0	−15	−29	−44	−59	−74	−88	−104
30	28	13	−2	−18	−33	−48	−63	−79	−94	−109
35	27	11	−4	−20	−35	−49	−67	−82	−98	−113
40	26	10	−6	−21	−37	−53	−69	−85	−100	−116
Wind speeds greater than 40 MPH have little added effect	Little Danger for properly clothed person		Increasing Danger			Great Danger				
			Danger from freezing of exposed flesh							

Dress Properly for the Trip

Choosing appropriate clothing for the existing conditions is very important. Man is warm-blooded and only survives in cold climates because he uses his imagination and ingenuity to find ways to maintain appropriate body temperature. Most people must maintain a total exposure temperature from 75 to 100 degrees. People differ in how they react to cold and your choice of clothing must be geared to your own reactions.

Clothing insulates the body from the cold environment and protects it from wind and moisture. If the torso is warm enough, excess heat which is generated in the form of energy is directed to the extremities that have less protection.

Even though fashion influences the way we dress, sometimes it does not accomplish the task of maintaining warmth. It is important that the style of dress prevents body perspiration from getting into the clothing. The clothes must provide for ventilation of body moisture. Thermal underwear is one of the best answers to this, however it must *never* be worn next to the skin as it does not effectively absorb perspiration. Holes in outer wear often allow for the evaporation of body moisture but also may let moisture in.

If you find you are wearing too much clothing for the conditions, uncover your head first, after that open the neck and let the warm air out from the torso area. Opening the wrists allows cool air to get to the greater perspiring areas of the body—the axillae.

The materials used by manufacturers to insulate clothing are goose and duck down and nylon. Goose down, by its very nature of creation, seems to be the finest insulation against extreme cold. Nylon, although cold to the touch, has a low heat-loss capacity and conducts warmth well. It also absorbs very little body heat, has less bulk and protects against wind.

Hands and feet are very difficult to protect. Ski gloves are not suggested for snowmobiling as they have been designed to curve around ski poles and tend to stretch very tightly over the knuckles. Wool mittens provide more protection than gloves, especially when they are covered with a wind- and moisture-proof covering of nylon. New designs of synthetic hand coverings are being tested and may someday revolutionize the glove industry. Their biggest problem now is that of bulk. The feet support body weight and are farthest from the torso, where most heat is generated. Wool socks in leather boots provide the best protection. Felt makes the best insole, and most snowmobile boots on the market have this feature.

With our present knowledge of anatomy and physiology there is no reason why manufacturers cannot create sensible fashions for snowmobiling that are not only good looking and comfortable, but do the job they were intended to do: maintain body warmth.

The most suitable clothing for both racing and recreation snowmobiling is the one-piece coverall. As designers study the problems of the two- and the one-piece suit they tend to agree that the one-piece garment provides greater warmth. Most outfits are made of a closely woven nylon fabric that resists wind penetration and is treated to resist tears and moisture. The quilting stitch has been found to allow moisture to penetrate into the lining, and most quilting is now done only on the inner lining. The degree of insulation is based on thickness and because there is little physical activity involved in driving or riding on a snowmobile, the garment must be thicker than the usual winter wear. The better garments have a goose down interior covered by a synthetic polyester with a fleece lining.

The biggest problem of two-piece outfits is draft air. Manufacturers find that by lengthening the jacket and raising the pants, draft is less a problem. Most garments have knit wristlets and adjustable belts. Leg zippers allow the pants to be snug against the leg, and pockets have snaps or zippers to keep snow out. Drawstrings around the hood keep the head and neck from losing warmth, and any fur trim is strictly for looks.

Proper attire for snowmobilers should include a warm garment, a helmet for head protection, goggles that protect the eyes from wind, snow, and obstacles, and gloves that allow the driver to grip the handlebars without cutting off circulation. The boot should have waterproof nylon uppers and a drawstring, rubber bottoms, and a removable felt inner that may be taken out and allowed to dry if wet. Most outfits match the color of the snowmobile, but some manufacturers list as many as ten different colors.

If it is extremely cold a face mask of wool or a balaclava provides protection for the face. Be choosy about your clothing and remember it is important for your morale to look good, but it is more sensible to feel good.

Transporting the Snowmobile to the Destination

Most snowmobiles must travel to a scramble area and thus transport their vehicle by trailer. Usually there is no problem and the transportation may be made simply and safely by following these suggestions.

1. Be certain that the weight of the trailer and snow-

mobile does not outweigh the car or truck pulling it (for example, don't use a compact car to haul a two- or three-rig trailer).

2. Cars with automatic transmission give a smoother, less jerky ride especially when attempting a steep grade.

3. If possible have the car equipped with a load-leveling hitch that distributes the weight so the car and trailer share the pulling burden.

4. Avoid too much weight on the trailer tongue.

5. Tilt beds allow easy access to the trailer and a swivel tongue lets you move the trailer to the best possible position for disengagement.

6. Have a safety coupler to prevent separation in motion.

7. Locks on the axle will prevent most thefts.

8. Trailers must have taillights.

9. Louvered ridges give traction to the snowmobile during loading and unloading.

10. Note the load capacity and never exceed its limit.

11. Stabilizing jacks allow for safe parking. If the trailer has one, use it.

12. Before you leave for your trip, check to see that the vehicle is properly secured onto the trailer with rope or straps.

In the Appendix there is a list of 31 manufacturers who build trailers especially for snowmobiles.

Most snowmobile trailers start at $125 and may manage a weight load of at least 750 pounds. The basic design is similar to a tilted boat trailer except that there is a flat bottom instead of a "V." Trailers are designed to transport up to four vehicles. Most are extremely rugged, built of steel, and lightweight.

When unloading the snowmobile, a release clamp enables the trailer to tilt the rear downward and to one side so the vehicle can be driven off. Be careful not to press the throttle too much as it will not only jerk the vehicle off but may also damage the rubber drive belt. When loading, the release clamp is used to bring the rear of the bed down so the machine may be driven slowly up to the edge and onto the bed. A little practice makes this procedure quite simple. Once the vehicle is on the bed it should be anchored with rope or specially designed rubber and chain attachments. If the vehicle is not secured it may slide off while being transported. It is recommended to use the rubber straps, as ropes not only are time consuming but usually insufficient. Some trailers come with a steel bar that fits across the skis and holds the vehicle securely.

Sleighs are a little more difficult to load and unload as they have no power themselves and in most cases must be pulled on. But because they are lightweight they usually provide no difficulty.

Trail Markings

If you are planning to use a state or national park or a private trail you must become familiar with the various markings that are intended to keep you on a designated path for your safety and enjoyment. The state of Vermont has the signs shown below. Check your state for variations.

ON TRAIL   INTERSECTION   DA

By 1972 it is hoped that standard signs will appear: an orange reflective diamond 5 x 7 inches for trail blazers and a 9 x 12 for directional symbols.

Wildlife

In the winter months most animals and birds have a difficult time struggling for their lives without being harassed by snowmobiles. Many states provide winter yards and refuges for the protection of these animals. For most deer and moose, evergreens are the basic wintertime food supply and also act as shelter. It is imperative that snowmobilers do not destroy these trees by careless driving.

Dogs are hazards to most wild animals, and since snowmobiling has become so popular they have learned to use the tracks that snowmobiles leave to obtain easy access into the forest. Do not travel close to yards or refuges or even known herd areas because of the threat to these animals by dogs. Never chase animals, as it may mean certain death for them if they become exhausted and unable to search for food. Most state and national parks and forests impose strict fines and other penalties for such harassment.

Accessories for the Trip

There are so many accessories for snowmobiles that any list today would be obsolete tomorrow. As the sport grows and needs become evident, some manufacturer will come along to fill the need and make the sport more enjoyable.

The most popular accessory is the snowmobile sled, which enables more people, especially families, to "go along for the ride." There are numerous companies who produce sleds in all shapes, sizes, and colors. They are made of wood, steel, aluminum, or fiberglass. Some look like an Alaskan dogsled and others are small replicas of Santa's sleigh. More modern manufacturers shape them like torpedoes, sidecars, and speed boats. Whatever style you select there is one thing sure: the sled broadens enjoyment of the sport and its use is almost limitless. If you don't use the sled to transport people you can use it to haul camping supplies, firewood, tools, or anything that is not nailed down. In the Appendix is a list of sleigh manufacturers.

Other popular accessories include such things as:

Sleds with hatches in the bottom for ice fishing

Wheel kits for using the snowmobile in the summer

Engine modification component kits for those interested in high speed for racing

Extra instruments—gauges, dials—for an already packed dashboard.

Although some states forbid their use, there are exhaust megaphones

Tinted windshields to cut down on glare

Built in camera settings

Protective covers or cabs

Canvas covers

Snowshoes to match your vehicle

Duffle bags to match your vehicle

Coasters and ashtrays

Kidney belts to eliminate fatigue on long safaris

Saddlebags to carry the extras

Trail survival kits

Helmets for head protection

Timing devices for engines

Speedometer kits

Head temperature gauge to protect the engine against overload and overheating

Special field glasses

Electric start kits

Skid-proof kits to aid in steering

Sheds and tents that are compact

Tacometer kits

Special jacks

Tote bags

Gas primer kits

Rivet kits

Ice stud kits

Wheel kits

Deep snow skid frames

Boat conversion kits

Power tuned mufflers

Sitting skis (a skier sitting on one ski is pulled behind a snowmobile)

Electric meat smoker

Special portable heaters

Caps with special safety features

Hand warmers

Electric socks

Body warming belts

Accessories all add to comfort and pleasure and assist in planning for the trip.

10

National Parks

"The National Park System is dedicated to conserving the scenic, scientific and historic heritage of the United States for the benefit and enjoyment of its people." In 1916 the National Park Service was created by an act of Congress, with Stephen T. Mather appointed as director. National forests are maintained by the Department of Agriculture and were established in 1905. The National Park Service is a branch of the United States Department of the Interior and urges snowmobilers to become familiar with the national park and forest system, which is the actual property of all Americans. Although the service does not provide any publications concerning trails and rules for snowmobile operation, it does give information through the Director of Recreation, United States Department of Agriculture, Forest Service, Washington, D.C. 20250.

The season for snowmobiling is governed only by the amount of snow covering the ground in national parks and forests. When snow is insufficient, trails will be closed. For accommodations there are a few hotels, lodges, and camps, but these are located on adjoining private land. In most areas the demand for accommodations exceeds the number available so it is recommended to make reservations ahead of time.

The National Park Service maintains campsites, which may be used without any charge; however, some parks do charge a small admission fee.

Presently there are 201 national parks and monuments and 154 national forests, which cover over 300 million acres in 50 States and Puerto Rico. Where conditions permit, snowmobiles are allowed to be operated as long as all established rules of park conduct are followed. The National Forest Service is in the process of creating a code of conduct for snowmobilers.

Recently the Federal Government has instigated a program called "Operation Golden Eagle." This program calls for the fee of $7 for entrance permits, which goes into a general fund to be used for the improvement of parks and forests. These permits may be obtained by writing the United States Bureau of Outdoor Recreation, Box 7763, Washington, D.C. 20044. Beside the certificate you will also receive a Golden Eagle lapel pin and family award certificate. The entrance permit does not eliminate the fee that is charged in some areas for other special services.

Snowmobiling in National Forests and Parks can be a thrilling experience. Each forest has its own particular pattern. Foresters plant new crops of trees to replace yearly harvested ones, which constantly give rise to new adventures year after year.

Once snow has covered the ground sufficiently for snowmobile use, national foresters put up their welcome signs. In the snow belt areas (shown on the following map) the

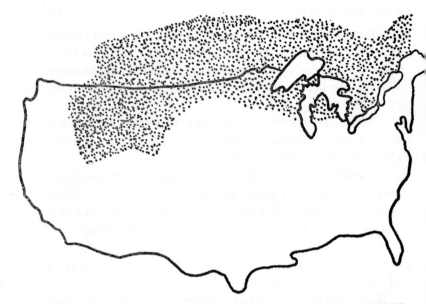

RECOMMENDED SNOW BELT FOR PERMANENT TRAIL CONSTRUCTION
Average Annual Snow Cover of 100 Days or More (1″ or More). (Atlanta, Georgia, Conway Publication, Inc., 1963. *The Weather Handbook*, by H. M. Conway Jr., p. 219.)

parks and forests have about 100 days available for snowmobiling.

In some mountain areas, the snowmobilers must be aware of dangerous avalanche conditions, such as in Wasatch National Forest, Alta, Utah. This mountain valley once became the graveyard of 120 people at a ski area. Alta now studies the weather daily during the winter months and when conditions exist that might create an avalanche, the forest rangers use a 75 mm recoilless rifle or a 2-pound block of TNT to test snow stability or artificially create an avalanche under safe controlled conditions. Rangers are presently studying the use of snowmobiles in national forests and are learning what measures they must take to make the sport as safe as possible.

The plans for forming a rescue snowmobile patrol will soon be a reality. In March of 1965, in Yellowstone National Park, 250 snowmobiles were admitted to the park. At that time no safe routes had been established and the ski patrol noted many harrowing experiences, which became an impetus to the formation of a snowmobile patrol. It was felt these patrolmen must not only be highly trained in snowmobiling but also in areas of mountain climbing, survival, avalanche control, and skiing. They must also know their park extremely well and maintain and inspect trails regularly.

Winter camping in national parks is becoming much more popular since the advent of snowmobiling. Whether the camping trip is for one day or one week, snowmobilers are finding this an inexpensive way to see the beauty of national parks and forests. In national parks all campsites are marked and most campers must have reservations. When the park is full the rangers will hang out a "Campground Full" sign and snowmobilers must make other accommodations.

The only way to get lost in a national park is to wander off the scheduled trail. Before you begin your adventure check to see that you know and understand the snowmobile signs, and be aware of them while you are on your trip. Be sensible and think safe.

If you are planning a snowmobile trip in the near future and would like to make before-trip preparations, start by writing the park or forest of your choice. There is probably one not far from you. A list of national parks and forests that allow snowmobiling can be found in the Appendix.

11

State Parks

A state park is "a relatively spacious area of outstanding scenic or wilderness character, oftentimes containing also significant historical, archaeological, economical, geological, and other specific values, preserved as nearly as possible in their original or natural condition and providing opportunity for appropriate types of recreation where such will not destroy or impair the features and values to be preserved."[3]

With the rapid growth of snowmobiling, concerned people are faced with a prominent problem that has been created within each state. Where can snowmobiles be driven so they will not only be safe but will allow for the greatest enjoyment of the sport?

State parks have actually been in existence since 1921 when Stephen T. Mather, first director of National Parks Service, encouraged the creation of a state park movement. At this time only 13 states had any type of park. Today

---

[3] Tilden, Freeman. *The State Parks.* Alfred A. Knopf, distributed by Random House, 1962, p. 11.

all states have parks covering over six million acres and costing taxpayers about 150 million dollars a year to maintain. On the other hand these parks have an estimated 300 million visitors yearly.

Despite rapid advances in the growth of state parks, the demand for use far outnumbers the places available. By the year 2000 there is estimated that the population of the United States will be 500 million. This doubles the population figure of 1950. Will these people have twice the time for recreation, twice the amount of money to spend on recreation, twice the number of hours away from their labor, and will they be able to travel twice as far for their recreation? Will their need for recreational activities be twice as great? These are the questions that government officials are concerned with in making long range plans for state parks and recreation areas.

Most state parks were created as a result of philanthropic donations. In Michigan, 59 of the first 64 parks were established by the donation of funds from interested persons and corporations. Some states have obtained park land by bond issue and some by special tax assessment.

State parks lure thousands of snowmobilers to their spacious areas. The majority of people come for their scenic or wilderness character. In most states the only recreation that is not allowed is hunting by snowmobile.

Using private and public land for the planning and mapping of snowmobile trails within each state has just begun on a large scale. It is hoped that some consistency of regulations can be created from state to state. Currently there is effort being directed toward uniform trail marking. A federal committee has been appointed to study the possibility of uniform marking consisting of the International Snowmobile Trails and Sign Committee and the

Inter-agency Task Force Committee. It is hoped that a manual of snowmobile signs and symbols will be created that will influence their use in all state parks.

State after state is developing policies for the use of snowmobiles within their boundaries. Below is the Michigan Motorized Snow Traveler Park Policy #23, courtesy of the Michigan Department of Parks and Recreation.

These particular types of motorized equipment are a wonderful boon to the outdoorsman or recreationist for use in the northern part of the state. When there is from three to five feet of snow to cushion the land, they do little damage.

Their use in some parts of Michigan can result in damaging the landscape when snow conditions are inadequate.

At times there just is not enough snowfall to protect the topsoil, seedlings and plant life to permit this kind of traffic.

Therefore, the following policy will govern the use of these vehicles in park and recreation areas:

1. Snow travelers may be operated only upon designated trails or areas. Such trails or areas will be properly signed for this use.

2. Snow travelers will be permitted to operate upon designated trails when there is sufficient snow to protect the ground surface. They will be permitted in snowmobile areas when there is a minimum of four inches of snow.

3. Snow travelers will not be permitted within dedicated nature study areas, nature reservations, research areas, sanctuaries or scenic sites.

4. Rallies, races, endurance meets or other organized competitive events will not be allowed. Requests to conduct such activities should be referred to the Division Office.

5. Motor vehicle permits will be required for snow traveler machines using the marked trails or snowmobile

areas when such trails or areas fall within any part of any area that is included in the Motor Vehicle Permit Law.

6. Motorized snow travelers shall be interpreted as vehicles equipped with belt drives, tracks and steered by skis or runners and registered as a snowmobile. Wheeled vehicles will not be permitted at any time even though they may be registered as a snowmobile.

7. All trails and areas will be marked with signs saying "Wheeled vehicles prohibited."

Trails: Trails which may include roads closed to vehicular traffic that are permissible for snow traveler use will be recommended by the park supervisor through channels. All trails must have approval of Parks Division Office prior to any construction activity or permissive use.

Signs: Trail signs or symbols will be used to mark and identify such approved trails.

Snowmobile areas: Snowmobile areas may be selected by Division Office on an experimental basis to determine the impact of such use upon the environment of parks that have varying snow conditions. Such areas will be established on a limited basis after consultation with the field staff. Such areas may or may not become permanent.

Enforcement: Arrests will be made or a summons issued when marked trails or areas are available and snowmobiles trespass into areas which are not open to such use. Arrests will be made or a summons issued when snowmobiles trespass within parks that have no designated snowmobile trails or areas.

Temporary Trails: Upon requests of groups or organizations, and where snow conditions permit, trails may be laid out by the park supervisor using poles and cloth flags if approved by the Division office. Such requests will be handled by mail or telephone through regular channels depending upon the time available. The basic judgment factor must be the protection of the land, seedlings, and plant life. Markers will be removed when activity is completed.

Motor Vehicle Permits: Permits will be required for

snow traveler machines using the marked trails or areas when such trails or areas fall within any part of any area that is included in the Motor Vehicle Permit Law. Revised 1-16-70.

If more information is needed as to what public land is available for snowmobiling, it might be wise to contact your state snowmobile association. See the Appendix for a list.

Generally state parks have no admission fees, but some do charge for parking, camping, and snowmobile registration. The State Tourist Council, listed in the Appendix, will provide interested persons with information as to events in parks, guides to trails, points of interest, historic signs, zoos, shelters, herd areas, hunting rules and regulations, and other recreational facilities including rest and camping sites. If you plan on going to another state, write ahead to find out any out-of-state regulations.

12

Family Snowmobiling and Camping

An afternoon of snowmobiling can turn an ordinary winter day into a happy family holiday. There are so many places that offer something for everyone, and probably the biggest problems families will have is where to go and what exactly to do.

What is very thrilling is to seek out a summer hide-away and find out what it looks like in the winter. Most likely the familiar summer resort you once visited now has snowmobile facilities. Of all the accessories available to make snowmobiling more exciting don't forget the family camera. If you find you have more equipment and people than you have places to put them you might fasten a toboggan onto the back of the sleigh to carry those needed extras.

Fortunate are the families who own or have access to a summer cottage. With a little work here and there most summer homes can be converted for winter. Antifreeze poured into the drains will prevent pipes from freezing and enable the sink and toilet to be used. If you have a large jug for drinking water, bring it along; otherwise boil snow. A roaring fire and a warm sleeping bag supply the basic needs of food and shelter.

Family groups are uniting all over to form family clubs, which plan trips and activities to meet the needs of all members. Some find that racing appeals to them, and they combine a weekend of racing with a family get-together. No matter where your interest lies, there is something for you and your snowmobile. Some states have organized cruises that are open to snowmobile clubs or private groups.

Night snowmobiling is becoming more popular, and sights and sounds of a winter night can hardly be matched. Families find that after their day's work has come to an end and the dinner dishes are put away, an invigorating snow cruise is about the best way to prepare for a good night's sleep.

If a family would like to find out what snowmobiling is like before making the investment, there are a growing number of private concerns who rent snowmobiles by the hour, day, or week. However, just one day of snowmobiling is enough to instill the incentive to have equipment of your own.

Snowmobiling promotes the importance of family togetherness. It gives all members of the family a renewed feeling of security and belonging. Getting along with others seems to be a prominent problem in our society. Some sociologists feel that the inability to get along with family members is one reason why people cannot get along in other social situations. Sports, no matter what kind, teach how to give and take, and snowmobiling gives families a chance to practice this necessary social phenomenon.

Snowmobiling can be the source of similar family interests. Making plans and working together toward a common goal makes for strong family ties. The family is the foundation of society and its functioning must not be allowed to deteriorate. Snowmobiling has helped to strengthen family bonds and is an asset to society.

There is an enormous assortment of winter wilderness activities for families, and snowmobiling gives many opportunities to combine itself with the associated activities of camping. Once the campsite has been selected, snowmobile safaris, snowshoeing, hiking, ice skating, ice fishing, hunting, skijoring, and even skiing can be enjoyed.

Families who camp must first be interested in outdoor living and must know the techniques of camping as well as cold-weather survival. They should also enjoy being a part of a well-organized team and accepting responsibilities. Other qualifications for the winter-time camping family are:

1. Some summer camping experience.

2. Skills of packing, open-fire cooking, fire making, wood gathering, wood chopping, tent or shelter construction, map and compass reading, trail reading, and use of water.

3. Area familiarity. Knowing the area is very important because the winter changes the landscape a great deal.

4. Knowledge of first aid with extra knowledge of possible winter hazards.

5. Possession of appropriate equipment.

6. Knowledge of the associated activities that are planned for the trip, as well as being a safe snowmobiler.

Families must be prepared for their camping experience and must have adequate and appropriate equipment and clothing (see Chapter 8 for clothing). For a one-day trip, an overnight stay, or a week of camping, pre-trip preparations should include the following:

1. Preparation of the snowmobile.
2. Provisions for food, water, shelter, sleeping, and body elimination.
3. Appropriate clothing.
4. Schedule or plan of the trip, which is made in duplicate and left with a responsible person. This plan should designate where all stops will be made and approximate time of arrival and departure.

Camping Shelter

After the campsite has been reached, the first task is to establish shelter. Organization is of prime importance, and every member should have a specific responsibility. The shelter should be one that is not exposed to wind and snow, and it should have some type of a natural windbreak. If a tent is to be erected, the area should first be packed down either by foot or by the snowmobile. The opening of the tent should face away from any winds and the fire should be built in front of the opening. If the tent has a steep pitch, and there is a possibility of snow, move the fire a little farther than usual from the tent to avoid snow extinguishing it. An important point to remember is that the campsite must be kept dry. The snow in the tent area must not melt; therefore it is wise to have boughs, bushes, or even a large tarpaulin under the tent floor. If the tent becomes encrusted with ice crystals use a bough to whisk them away. Even though the tent is pitched away from wind and snow it is not wise to put it directly under trees heavily laden with snow. It should be in a little sunlight, as the sun will warm it during the day. Don't place your tent too close to any highway or snowmobile trail. Safety and comfort are good reasons for keeping the campsite away from moving traffic.

Know how to pitch your particular tent. If you have difficulty getting stakes into the ground after you have chipped away a stake hole and inserted the stake, pack the area with ice and snow. It is a good idea to carry extra rope for extra support if the need arises. If you are camping in an underdeveloped or wilderness area be sure of the location and mark it on your map. Know how to use your compass (See Chapter 17).

Some snowmobile camping is done with trailers and campers, which provide the greatest amount of comfort. All the basic necessities are built in. The family will have to decide what they want. Basically tents are less expensive, are easy to erect, and do not require a lot of storage area. Trailer and campers provide all the modern conveniences, but they are limited to areas where autos drive and require a little maneuvering. Some trailers are expensive. If you are not a hardy breed, tent camping is not for you. Choose a trailer.

Sleeping Arrangements

If your winter camping experience requires you to sleep overnight in a tent or trailer, the first requirement to a happy night's sleep is comfort. Warmth is the first ingredient. Modern camping gear for sleeping takes the form of sleeping bags. They come in an array of sizes, colors, and comfort features—even electric. When selecting a sleeping bag be sure that it is waterproof, even if you plan on sleeping in a camper. Always carry along extra blankets and put as many under you as over you.

Modern camping must include some type of mattress or cot. Most are inexpensive and well worth the investment. Rubber mattresses will last longer than plastic ones, and both are easy to inflate and store.

If you will be sleeping in a camper or trailer you may even choose to sleep in beds made up with sheets depending on the heating ability of the trailer or camper. Again be sure to have extra blankets in case something goes wrong.

Fires

Campfires are the most wonderful aspect of winter camping. They are used for cooking, heat, and light, and they act as a focal point of the campsite.

Some campsites offer very little material for firewood because they are usually wet. It might be a good idea to bring along a few dry pieces of kindling and tinder to get and keep the fire going. Cedar and pine make the best quick-starting fuel for fires as they burn rapidly. If you plan on keeping the fire going all night you might add charcoal. The harder woods—hickory, oak, and maple—will burn a long time but are difficult to get started.

While making your fire be careful not to catch the evergreens on fire. A wintertime forest fire can be very dangerous. When looking for wood be careful if you are cutting a dead tree down. The tree may be rotten inside and may break off and fall on you.

Most parks and forests have fireplaces that are ready for use; all you need to do is add fuel.

Cooking

There is no other taste that can match a well-cooked open-fire meal, no matter what is served. Being out-of-doors in the winter gives an added longing to replace the energy expelled in activity and a good cooked meal is the highlight of any camping experience. If you want to boil water, make a high hot fire; if you want to cook meat or other foods, wait until the coals are red hot. Aluminum foil is a boon to open-fire cooking, and almost anything can be cooked in it (however, the open fire taste will be eliminated). The hunter's fire is the best style for winter fires.

If you build a fire for warmth, some type of reflector helps to direct the heat where you want it to go.

When planning the winter meals it is advisable to select foods that eliminate the use of pots and pans. Refrigeration will not be a problem but keeping cooked food warm may. Hot drinks are in order for a cold winter day and most of these drinks come in powdered form. All you need is hot milk or water.

Foods should be in their dryest form. Most will be dehydrated or powdered because they take less storage space and are the easiest to prepare. It is the wise camper who takes along energy foods containing sugar for added strength on the trail and in camp. Candy is recommended. Here is a list of necessary cooking and eating supplies:

1. lightweight pans or aluminum foil
2. paper plates and cups

3. napkins and plastic bags
4. plastic silverware
5. sharp knives
6. dish rag, or sponge, and towel
7. water jug
8. can opener
9. mixing container
10. cooking forks

After the menu has been created, other special equipment needed for that particular food should be added.

Most camping trips require from one to six meals. The longer your trip the larger the number of meals and greater the amount of equipment. Wintertime camping means extra warm equipment, so it is important to plan very simple meals. Do not overload the snowmobile sleigh or toboggan and take only essential items.

Water will not be a problem as snow can easily be melted. However, while melting it, stir occasionally to prevent scorching. Water-purifying tablets are available at drug stores, and even though the water is boiled it should be purified. You will never know when you will need water, so keep a can on or near the fire at all times while in the camp.

Cleaning up after your meals should also be simple—throw it all away. If you use cans as pots throw them away, as you will have more cans at your next meal. It is not wise to save food that has been opened so try to use only the amount you will need for that particular meal. Be careful about touching cold metal with your hand and mouth as they may freeze directly to the metal causing pain and injury.

Consider the following foods for your winter camping trip:

bread
butter or margarine
sugar
salt
pepper
seasoning
instant coffee, tea, cocoa
catsup
mustard
jam or jelly

peanut butter
powdered milk
cheese
eggs
instant or canned potatoes
dry cereal
potato chips
soup
canned meat dishes

canned or dried fruits
canned vegetables
bacon or ham
lunchmeats
hot dogs
meat
crackers and cookies
marshmallows
candy and nuts

For your winter camping holiday also consider the following equipment:

standard ax
hand ax or hatchet
shovel
large knife
digging tool
water container
cooking stove
portable refrigerator
rope
string
towels
wash basin
extra batteries

lamp, lantern, and flashlight
sleeping bags
tent
tarpaulin and plastic sheets
clock
toilet tissue
air mattress or cots
repair kits
change of clothes
toys for children
matches and candles
compass
map
first aid and survival kit

If you are packing your camping equipment onto a sleigh or toboggan for the snowmobile to pull you may eliminate extra equipment for cooking, but never those things necessary for warmth.

Finally here are a few special features of winter camping that snowmobilers must consider:

1. Tent fabrics and rope may shrink when wet.

2. Holes may occur in tent fabrics if the frozen material is struck.

3. Snow may load up on a tent top, so keep it as clear as possible.

4. If an unexpected snowstorm occurs pile tree boughs against the side of the tent and park the snowmobile or sleigh on the side the wind is coming from.

5. Unusual cold may mean sleeping in two sleeping bags, one inside the other. More clothing should be worn, even a cap.

6. Wood for your fire should be protected with a waterproof material.

7. If you fall into water, or become wet, roll in the snow, which will absorb a great deal of moisture and save you from freezing.

8. Sunglasses should be worn on sunny days because of the excess glare.

9. When muscular activity decreases, the body's ability to produce heat decreases and the individual must be aware of possible freezing or frostbite. Fatigue and regional pain must never be overlooked.

10. The wintertime snowmobile camper must be in top physical shape because survival takes extra strength, power, and endurance. Be fit *before* your trip.

13

Snowmobile Clubs

The popularity and growth of snowmobiling as a sport has also brought an equally rapid growth in the development of snowmobile clubs. More than 10,000 clubs (many independent) have been created since 1960, mostly in small towns across the upper portion of the United States and throughout Canada. An increasing number of clubs are joining national organizations that add to their activities by providing various services for their benefit.

The purpose of most clubs, as exemplified by the Owosso, Michigan, Sno-Scramblers, is to "promote friendship and good will, to protect and promote the best interests of the members both individually and as a group, and to offer assistance to the general public and law enforcement agencies in case of emergency." If your area desires to form a club and does not know how to begin, here are a few pointers:

1. Set the objectives you want your group to achieve.
2. Contact interested persons whose cooperation can be enlisted.

3. Through the various forms of mass media, contact the public.

Before any public action is taken, persons interested in organizing a snowmobile club should call a preliminary meeting that should formulate policies and a general plan for action, which should include a public meeting for final organization. Keep in mind the necessity of positive public relations and be sure events and activities are made public. Some methods of attracting public attention are lectures, exhibits, demonstrations, snowmobiling schools, mass meetings, motion pictures and slides, and special events. Methods of reaching the public are newspapers, radio, movies and television. At this meeting the group must decide which methods are the most effective. Help might be obtained from already established clubs, from such organizations as the United States Snowmobile Association, or from material distributed through dealers such as "How to Organize for More Winter Fun," by Evinrude Motors.

In some areas the drive to organize the club could be made through an already existing group such as Rotary, Kiwanis, local ski clubs, or municipal recreation groups. Of course the greatest success will be the result of good leadership. At the preliminary meeting, officers and a board of directors are elected and jobs designated. At the first general meeting, the goals and objectives are explained, committees give reports and persons are enlisted to help. The meeting should be short so that interest and enthusiasm can crystallize into some definite action. Resolutions should be made and plans for activities and membership decided upon.

Below are a number of points that must be considered when organizing a snowmobile club.

1. The club must have homogeneous (similar) interests.
2. The club should be organized with permanent status in mind.
3. Organization should include sound business methods.
4. Officers who are competent should be chosen democratically.
5. The club must be active enough to have an influence on the community.
6. The club should offer its members an attractive program of snowmobiling activities.
7. There should be some sort of snowmobiling education program included in the activities.
8. The club should encourage the perfection of snowmobiling ability and encourage safe driving habits.
9. Information of club activities should be made in sufficient time for members to make plans.
10. Total fitness (not only physical) should be encouraged and programs to obtain this fitness planned for.
11. Safe snowmobiling rules should be available to all members.
12. A snowmobile patrol should be created and all members educated in the rudiments of first aid.
13. Information on competitive events as well as safaris and rallies should be made available.
14. Information about other clubs and organizations should be made available.
15. The club should take a stand on improving equipment. Informing companies of unsafe items is one way to further this point.
16. The club should favor reliable snowmobile manufacturers as well as their dealers and repairmen. Records

should be kept of poor repair work and poor relations with snowmobile dealers.

17. The club should endeavor to create safe trails and to give information on private and municipal trails that offer good facilities.

18. The club should appeal to local, state, and federal sources for fair snowmobile legislation.

19. Reports of inadequate snowmobile operations should be reported to the proper authorities.

20. Information such as weather reports, snow conditions, and trail maps should be given regularly to all members.

21. The club should provide emergency service to the community when the need arises.

22. The club should make use of any service available to them from local, state, national, and private organizations.

23. The club should be responsible for formulating guidelines on proper snowmobile behavior.

24. The club should provide anyone interested in snowmobiling information on how to become involved in it.

25. Each club member should remember that he not only represents himself but his club and city. His behavior should be in the highest ideals of good sportsmanship.

As well as improving their local organization, snowmobile clubs should provide members with as many activities as there are interests and needs. The activities of the club, if well publicized, could encourage non-club snowmobilers to become interested in the group activities. Small clubs will find that they are limited in the activities they engage in because of membership and available funds.

Snowmobile Club Activities

Snowmobile Rallies

Almost any group can stage a successful snowmobile rally, but it takes planning, manpower, and hard work. It isn't easy, but it's a rewarding experience that can bring new business and public attention to your community. Who stages the rally isn't nearly as important as *how* the rally is staged. Success depends on hard work, and most of the benefits are self-evident. For dealers, it is a good way to build interest in snowmobiles. Towns benefit from increased traffic and local publicity. Service clubs can stage rallies as a means of raising funds. Snowmobile owners enjoy the spirited competition and the test of driving skill.

The first informational meeting can be held as much as eight months in advance, and a minimum of two months is recommended. It takes this long to organize your committees and begin the leg work. As many different groups and organizations as possible should be invited to this first meeting. This includes snowmobile dealers; community leaders and government officials, including the law enforcement agency; service clubs; newspaper, radio, and TV representatives; snowmobile club officials; and any other interested party.

A detailed agenda should be prepared, mimeographed, and distributed to everyone attending. This will establish guidelines for discussion. Discuss the size of the rally and how large the community wants to go: 20–40 snowmobiles —local event; 40–60 snowmobiles—regional event; 60–100 snowmobiles—major event. The size indicates the amount of work necessary. Temporary committee chairmen investigate service club support, possible rally sites, number of potential entrants, and the best date to hold the rally. Finally the date for the next meet when report will be heard and discussed will be set.

At the planning meeting chairmen should report their findings. Here are the necessary committees and their responsibilities:

GENERAL CHAIRMAN. The official spokesman who has over-all responsibility. He handles financial affairs, pays bills, and issues final reports on funds.

EXECUTIVE COMMITTEE. The chairmen of individual committees make up the membership. It acts as an advisory group and coordinates the efforts of all committees. It must pass on all final decisions made by committee chairmen.

RALLY SITE COMMITTEE. This group selects actual site of the rally and maps out general area and each race course. It is responsible for marking course clearly with flags, pennants, and signs.

EVENTS COMMITTEE. Selects events that will be staged and works with rally site committee to plan a challenging but safe course. This committee should include experienced snowmobile operators.

ENTRY AND REGISTRATION COMMITTEE. The members must establish entry fee—if any, print and distribute entry blanks, and conduct actual registration at rally.

RACE COMMITTEE. Experienced snowmobile operators and dealers should staff this committee. They must establish classes for competition and lay down all ground rules for competition—and make sure these rules are followed. They maintain the right to disqualify any snowmobile from competition.

SPECIAL EVENTS COMMITTEE. Selects and plans the number of special events that will be conducted during the rally.

PUBLICITY COMMITTEE. Prepares all news releases and makes arrangements for press coverage.

DEMONSTRATION AREA COMMITTEE. Establishes an area where dealers can give free demonstration rides.

SPECTATOR-PARKING COMMITTEE. Works closely with rally site and events committees to insure adequate spectator appeal. Arranges parking with cooperation of law enforcement agencies.

PRIZE COMMITTEE. Selects type and number of prizes to be presented.

Information on snowmobile rallies has been synopsized from "How to Stage a Snowmobile Rally," a pamphlet published by Evinrude Motors, Division of Outboard Marine Corporation, 4143 North 27th Street, Milwaukee, Wisconsin 53216.

Program of Instruction

When a person or family joins a snowmobile club it is assumed that they own a machine and have basic knowledge of its use. There are certain rules of snowmobile operation that this person does not know and will have to learn. The instruction program can be based upon the knowledge of certain members who are not only familiar with snowmobile operation but with laws of snowmobiling, trail riding, safari organization, and the rules of the specific club. Presently there are no certified instructors courses but there may be in the near future. The club should establish some type of standard proficiency test that all members must take.

Safety and First Aid

It is unfortunate indeed for a club not to have all its

members prepared for emergencies. Not only should members be trained in some kind of accident prevention program but they should at least know what to do until a physician arrives or an injured person reaches medical help. Members should try to keep up their American Red Cross first-aid card and become familiar with the emergencies associated with the winter climate. They should all have first aid equipment for their snowmobile and should know how to use it. If the club is interested in this aspect contact the nearest American Red Cross for information.

Programs for Junior Snowmobilers

Since most clubs are made up of family groups, the activities should include some type of junior program. Snowmobile drivers between the ages of 14 and 18 must not be forgotten. Clubs should encourage safe driving of junior snowmobilers and include such things as machine maintenance, first aid, accident prevention, and snowmobile operation. Adult members of the club should arrange for juniors to have access to the snowmobile, make sure they are dressed properly, supply access to scramble areas and racing sites, and provide them with some type of organized program. Activities within the club as well as between clubs should be planned regularly. State and national organizations do provide some supervised activities for this group, but it is better to have locally sponsored activities. Junior snowmobilers often gain valuable experience that enhances the caliber of the sport and brings recognition to the club.

Inter-club Activities

Many times there is a great deal of distance between clubs, and inter-club activities cannot be held very often.

However, when clubs are close, interaction will help strengthen both groups. Club activities could include special events, joint scrambles, overnight safaris, evening get-togethers, and some indoor social functions. Exchanging ideas and experience helps both groups. Having members attend such things as snowmobile conferences and sports shows will help make the club a more enjoyable experience for everyone. It would be wise for the club to subscribe to the various snowmobile magazines, just to keep up on what is new. Knowing where races are being held, where new facilities are located, and what new legislation has been passed is very important for local snowmobile clubs.

Competition

Although club racing is not as popular as individuals engaging in competition, more and more emphasis is being placed on this aspect. Some clubs have established a handicap system that enables slower machines to compete in an event with faster vehicles. Competition creates exciting interest in snowmobiling and the club racing chairman will find himself busier than ever each year. Clubs have found such things as "gag" races, slalom races, obstacle races, and conventional speed races to be a source of stimulation for new membership. Competition usually grows from local to state to national and finally international, with each member dropping out along the way as he sees fit. Some people need more competition than others and provisions to meet the needs of everyone should be made.

Club Reports

Some system of reporting activities and their results should be made. Many members cannot come to business meetings and some of the events so they must be notified as to what is forthcoming. A club newspaper (or dope sheet), a postcard, or even an article in the local newspaper could be the means of notifying members. During October through March a monthly report should be distributed in some way. Good publicity brings prestige to the snowmobile club and attracts new members as well.

Snowmobile Exchange

If the snowmobile suit gets too small, or if the machine gets too many miles on it, you might want to sell or swap, and club members should be notified. Snowmobiling is expensive and the cost may be cut a little. At the beginning of the snowmobile season it would be a good idea to have a "work Bee" to repair snowmobiles and maybe exchange clothing that you have outgrown over the summer. Make it a party—have a ball as well as prepare for the season ahead.

Snowmobile Club Lodges

If a club can arrange to have its own lodge and facilities it should never expect to make a profit from its club members. The lodge and facilities should be self-sustaining so it can meet all expenses, but your club will be seriously hurt if you attempt to turn the project into a money-making business. Membership fees should be as low as possible, and emphasis must be placed on recreational activities.

Off Season Activities

The activities that are held between seasons (camping and canoe trips, picnics, or hiking) keep the club together. The type of people who join the club will dictate the type of activities that will be sponsored during the off-season. Many clubs find social gatherings with dinner and dancing popular at the beginning and end of the season. Also pre-season get-togethers may also provide for some early planning of activities for the coming season.

Drill Teams

Each year snowmobile clubs are including drill team activities into their programs. These teams demand a great deal of planning, coordination, teamwork, and concentration. Once the drill team is organized it may offer presentations or may challenge another club. Teams consist of eight to 100 vehicles and need about five acres of open field. Teams should group the snowmobile colors for best appearance and appoint a drill master to direct the signals.

Most snowmobile clubs are organized as "Family Fun Clubs" with their activities directed toward families having fun together. Some groups have worked together to build a club lodge and many put in hours of time figuring out ways to make money to sponsor activities. One club, the Sno-Mobilers of East Jordan, Michigan, scheduled a safari for Michigan lawmakers so they might understand snowmobiling a little better before passing any laws. Much of the Michigan law concerning snowmobiling was a result of the experiences these legislatures had. Some clubs have limited their membership and have a waiting list of new members. Most clubs do affiliate with some state or national organization.

For more information on how to organize a snowmobile club, consult the pamphlet prepared by Evinrude Motors, "How to Organize for More Winter Fun."

14

Resorts and Trails

Dr. Karl G. Pearson, Director of Real Estate Education for the University of Michigan, made available interesting facts concerning the impact of snowmobiling on real estate investments in a report to Kneale Brownson, Editor of the *Michigan Snowmobiler:*

1. Snowmobiling's contribution to the economy will increase at a rapid rate.
2. Recreation real estate development in northern areas will increase as much as five times the present level in the next ten years.
3. Snowmobiling will be among the generating forces helping in the development of northern wilderness and contribute to one of the greatest resort developments in the world.
4. In addition to the revenue from machine sales and tourism by snowmobilers, the sport will act as one of the drawing cards for investment in resort property.
5. Resort development will include both private home construction and commercial developments.
6. Since there are immense areas of land that remain

virtually undeveloped for resorts, snowmobiling will serve as an added recreational attraction as well as a transportation media providing access to land that is now inaccessible.

7. People have more time for sports, and more money to spend on them, thus creating a demand for recreational facilities.

8. Investors are becoming more and more interested in the leisure activities field.

9. The Southern California Research Council predicts by 1985 there will be a 25-week vacation.

10. As well as longer vacations, early retirement will increase demands for recreation.

11. Second home ownership has become a trend because of the movement toward early retirement and longer vacations.

12. In Michigan, over 100,000 families own two homes.

13. Snowmobiling is a popular activity for the retiree as it is an activity he can enjoy without great exertion.

14. Real estate people believe there is a great need for more luxurious motor inns, restaurants, and entertainment facilities because snowmobiling tourists can afford better accommodations.

15. After snowmobilers have spent time in the northern wilderness they begin looking for more things to do and their own accommodations.

16. Investment real estate includes such things as condominium apartments, lodges, hotels, motels, motor inns, and rental cottages all with adjoining snowmobile trails.

Some snowmobile clubs now run their activities in association with motels and lodges. The motel business in the north, because of customer scarcity in the winter, was a losing proposition. However, snowmobiling has sparked the investment in motel-owned snowmobile trails and machine rental, and some motel owners have reported yearly gross incomes increasing over two thousand percent because of this added attraction.

Snow ranches are also becoming quite popular with some groups attempting to control areas with a franchise system. The ranch program attracts families with small children and offers a variety of family-centered activities. Families don't even need to own their own snowmobile.

In some northern towns, municipalities are assessing a snowmobile tax and use the funds for the development of local trails. The tax in most reported incidents is dependent upon the mill rate and ranges from $2.50 to $40, depending on the make and model of the machine. In addition, these city groups enhance their trails, which run through public parks and forests, with clubhouses and other accommodations of comfort. Some municipalities even sponsor snowmobile races to draw people to their town and add to the income of other businesses there. It is all becoming a snowmobile centered operation to bring life to dying winter towns. In the state of Minnesota, one municipality boasts of owning seven public snowmobile trails that are operated by the local parks and recreation departments.

Some snowmobile areas resemble ski areas in that they have accommodations complete with chalets, hillside trails with snack bars, and even racetracks with room for spectators. Many areas offer free snowmobile trails but make their profit from concessions and other luxuries. Some resorts offer large prizes for racing and draw many spectators as well as snowmobilers. People today have money to spend and want to spend it for recreation.

Private parks without housing facilities provide racing facilities and cruising trails for a small fee. Their activities are usually organized for weekends, but they do allow snowmobile use during the week at a less expensive rate.

The growth of resort areas in Minnesota and Michigan has been stimulated by Michigan snowmobile registration of 25,000 in the upper peninsula, which accounts for one snowmobile for every 12 persons and an increase in ownership of over 12,000 in just one year. Upper peninsula banks and credit agencies find their winter loans skyrocketing and now offer special snowmobile loans with easy payment plans.

Each year, more and more parks and forests are being opened for snowmobile use. With these openings comes an increase in facility use and an increase in the need for accommodations as well as special programs. Awareness to the need for facilities is almost as great as the need for the development of safe and adequate snowmobile trails. Snowmobiling has been under public attack recently by two national publications *Life* and *The Wall Street Journal*. The basis for this lies in the fact that the sport has grown so rapidly that misuse was caused by inadequate facilities. Industry, realizing its responsibility not only for producing the vehicles and accessories, but for being instrumental in obtaining facilities for use, has issued guidelines for snowmobile operation, sponsored clinics and conferences to encourage the creation of public and private facilities, spoken to organized groups responsible for recreation in support of snowmobiling activities, lobbied for adequate and fair legislation at the national, state, and local level, and provided research information to be published in popular publications showing the need for the continuance of this sport. Manufacturers have taken steps to disseminate their research in courses that stress the importance of individual and group responsibility in following snowmobiling rules and regulations.

More and more people and organizations are joining in the fight to make snowmobiling a suitable winter sport. Examples of interest is shown by:

The Maine Snowmobile Association in 1969 attempted to obtain 17 million acres of industrial-owned property from the Maine Paper Industry Association.

In Montana, the United States Forest Service, in cooperation with the Montana Chamber of Commerce, and the Bureau of Land Management developed a 125-mile snowmobile run from Boozeman, Montana to West Yellowstone National Park. Each organization took a responsibility in maintaining this trail and called it "The Big Sky Trail."

In New York, 500 miles of snowmobile trails were created in the 1969–1970 season for public use. In the Ray Brook conservation section, a conservation officer created a trail with lean-tos along the way to add to the safety and comfort of the sport. Snowmobilers could register their names, destination, time of departure, and estimated time of arrival—all of which would be checked upon by a voluntary search and rescue team.

Vermont organized a number of modern trails with accommodations in the vast northwest wilderness.

Minnesota maintains 13 state parks operated by the state conservation department and has organized numerous activities to meet the demands of snowmobiling. In Crookston, a snowmobile complex was created on a natural snowbowl, which included a chalet, a snack bar, lodging, and an oval track that would provide for 1500 spectators.

Iowa boasts of 20 state recreation areas in public parks and forests and expects snowmobiling to boom there in the next few years.

Wisconsin sponsored a survey which revealed that over half the ski areas in the state also had organized snowmobile activities. The combination of the sport tended to increase skiing activities 20 percent in some areas and decreased it 40 percent in others.

The Canadian Snowmobile Association in Ste. Agathe des Mts., Canada, toured their country to determine problems of snowmobiling. The information gained was distributed to the membership clubs who used the information to improve local conditions.

Pennsylvania cites a county park that charges a fee of $10 a season, which permits snowmobiles to use public trails.

South Dakota reports that park rangers, lumbermen, and ranchers use snowmobiles in their work, and the machines have opened up many remote wintertime areas.

In Michigan, a Clawson real estate firm is managing two lodges, one in the upper peninsula and one in the lower peninsula. The resorts offer winter snowmobiling and skiing and summer golf (300 owners in one lodge and 125 in the other). The lower peninsula lodge added private building sites within the property.

These are just a few of the examples of the growth of snowmobiling in various parts of the United States and Canada. Both public and private organizations have joined in the recreation boom of snowmobiling. In some cases both have united, for example in Wisconsin. In 1970 a joint project sponsored by a snowmobile dealer, the United States Forest Service, the Wisconsin Department of Conservation, the St. Regis Paper Co., a Wisconsin service club, and the Wisconsin Boy Scouts created, marked, and maintained a 100-mile trail through private property and the Nicolet National Forest. This example shows that with a little interest and a little work, groups in almost any community can join forces to create better snowmobile facilities. Here are a few tips on how to accomplish this.

1. Obtain community support by showing a need for such facilities and indicate how they will benefit the community.

2. Get the support of local influential groups (service clubs, chamber of commerce, YMCA, YWCA, etc.) .

3. Review local maps for the best location. Trails should use as much public property as possible. If the land belongs to the state or national government, the conservation department of the state or the United States Forest Service should be contacted.

4. Contact all land owners involved in the proposed trail site.

5. Review local laws and regulations to be sure the trail will not violate any rules.

6. Form a committee of interested persons, local groups, land owners, city officials.

7. After the group has been formed, create a model trail with rules and regulations and submit the model to local officials for consideration.

8. If you have any problems, the International Snowmobile Association or the International Industrial Snowmobile Association will help local groups.

9. After your model has been accepted and all legal points worked out, the committee should find committee chairmen for the various aspects of the trail's creation and maintenance: finance, construction, signs, maintenance, safety, improvements.

10. Create a board of directors and begin operations. Make adjustments as they arise. Below is a synopsis of a report on trail construction from the Proceedings of the International Snowmobile Conference held in Albany, New York, in 1969. Information pertinent to trail construction should be kept up to date and this is just a start.

Environmental Quality

Certain deficiencies in recreational planning concern the lack of recreating zoning with provision for rallying grounds, rest stops, and designated trails. Snowmobiling has intruded into winter big-game feeding grounds causing destruction of vegetation, scattering of litter, and excess motor noise. The committee on environmental quality recommends that when creating snowmobile areas, officials should consider the following:

1. Recreation zoning. There should be designated areas of varied terrain suitable for the sport of snowmobiling and other areas suitable for cross-country skiing and snow-shoeing. These areas would be so reserved to avoid conflict with each other and with other appropriate uses or other public values. Zoning for snowmobiles should be so planned to provide a buffer (topographic, vegetative, or distance factor) to minimize physical interference with other users of the surrounding land. Such zoning should include consideration of (a) scenic beauty, (b) residences, (c) wildlife habitat, (d) areas designated for non-motorized recreation, (e) fragile plant communities or cover types that are highly susceptible to damage from snowmobile activity, (f) designated areas for special events or activities, (g) noise affecting the enjoyment of other outdoor users and neighboring homes and communities.

2. Protection of critical wildlife habitat, including big-game "yards." Snowmobile routes should be designed to provide a buffer of not less than 0.25 miles between said route and big-game wintering grounds, or feed yards or other areas of habitat that are essential to one or more species of wildlife or a group of animals for food and/or shelter during the winter season.

3. Rallying or pursuit of wildlife. There should be es-

tablished enforceable laws that provide for prosecution of persons who rally or pursue game animals or other wildlife with the aid of a snowmobile.

4. Noise control. It is recommended there be established enforceable state regulations for restricting entry on public land to snowmobiles certified by the manufacturer or authorized inspection as having a decibel rating of not more than 50db at 50 feet.

5. State and federal research should be devoted to studying the effects of off-road vehicles on fish and wildlife, seedlings, and other natural resources, including such factors as noise and air pollution.

6. States should consider comprehensive, environmentally protective legislation and regulation of *other* off-road vehicles, as well as snowmobiles.

7. Snow cover. It is recommended that, by appropriate regulation, snowmobiling on public lands be prohibited at such times as the average snow cover on open ground is less than four inches.

Trails and Signs Design

The committee on trails and signs design believe that providing trails could not solve all the problems of snowmobiling, because people will still continue to seek non-trail areas. Even though a trail development program complete with restrictions is necessary, its success depends on how well people responsible for the trails police their activities. Multiple trails, which provide opportunities for hiking, horseback riding, etc., seem to add to the interest in planned trails. However, skiing should never be associated directly with snowmobiling.

Locating Trails

Consider first snow availability, types of use, and land ownership. It is recommended that trails be located in snow belt areas where a minimum of 100 pass with one or more inches of snow. Part-time snowmobile trails could be considered, but they must have tight trail management. To minimize expenses use unplowed roads and restrict all snowmobiling when there is less than four inches of snow. Agricultural land provides the most interesting trails. In semi-wilderness areas, trails should be limited because of safety and the impact on natural resources. When using private land permission of the owner must be obtained and rules of trespassing subject to legal action should be made clear. Penalties should be imposed when improper use is demonstrated. Unmanaged trails are difficult to control and should be only allowed on large unclassified public lands in the West.

Types of Trails

General use trails should be directed toward families and organized groups with the majority of public lands falling into this type. The general use trail should be one way loops no more than 30 miles long with alternate shorter routes available.

Rally courses should be developed on private lands by private groups. The courses should be three to five miles in length and planned over a variety of land types. Rally courses should provide warm-up areas, fuel, repair facilities, food concessions, spectator facilities, and rest rooms. Spectators and drivers should be kept separate.

Race tracks should also be private enterprise with exception to holding races on existing county or municipal tracks that could be converted for snowmobile use. One-quarter or one-half-mile oval track is recommended with the same support facilities as in rally courses. Do not hold races on frozen lakes.

Existing and Potential Trails

On public lands, snowmobile use should be limited to marked trails. The backbone of these trails are logging roads, firebreaks, unplowed roads, power lines, pipelines, and abandoned railroad grades. Whenever possible, existing public lands should be utilized, keeping land acquisition to a minimum. In some cases permission to assess public land may be necessary to obtain from private land owners. Public groups can lease or obtain easement for trail crossing. It is important to maintain positive relations with private land owners if the trail system is to make progress. Snowmobile groups should sponsor facilities with special events and leave construction and operation of facilities such as lodges, restaurants, and other services to private groups and individuals. It is advisable to have these services on leased public lands or adjacent private property.

Trail Design and Construction Specifications

Here are 13 guides for developing general use trails based on experience. Trails should be designed to make changes as they may become obsolete.

1. Trail length of 15 to 30 miles is desirable, 40 to 50 miles maximum, 5 to 10 miles minimum. Although two-way trails may be necessary under certain conditions, one-way loop trails with alternate shorter routes are recom-

mended for safety and economy in construction and maintenance. Liability insurance and protection against tort claims may make one-way trails mandatory.

2. Trail tread width should vary with topography and land characteristics. Trail widths of 10 feet are desirable, 6 feet minimum, and 15 feet maximum. Where two-way trails are necessary, the minimum trail width should be 15 feet.

3. Turning radius should be a minimum of 25 feet.

4. Both vertical and horizontal sight distance should be a minimum of 50 feet. Snowbanks at road crossings should be cut back at least 500 feet in both directions, both sides. Snowbanks should be kept low at crossing points to permit easy exit from and entrance back on to the trail.

5. Grades and slopes should be a maximum of 25 percent. The in-run should be straight and at least as long as the slope. Sustained grades should be less, but sufficient engineering data is not available to make a specific recommendation.

6. A height of 10 feet above normal maximum snow accumulation should be cleared. Brush should be removed from the area 2 feet outside the edge of the trail.

7. Strict control of trail access points is highly recommended. Trails should be routed away from the areas that will attract undesirable traffic or uses.

8. Topography and land characteristics should be varied to maintain interest of the user, who can take advantage of outstanding scenic, historical, natural and educational features along the trail routes. Spur routes into interesting areas are recommended rather than running the main trail directly to the feature.

9. Occasional open areas should be provided for frolic

and rest. Trash barrels and picnic facilities may be included at these openings.

10. Trail maintenance is extremely important to improve trail usability and enjoyment. Constant clearing and rolling or dragging of the trail is needed to eliminate moguls (humps). Ideally, heavily used trails should be rolled immediately after each new snowfall.

11. Do not route snowmobile trails over lakes, streams, or other bodies of water. If stream crossings are necessary, provide bridges at least 8 feet wide made of material capable of retaining snow cover.

12. Trails should cross contours at right angles where possible. Routing trails along side slopes should be avoided.

13. Route trails away from game preserves, winter browse areas, experimental stations, nurseries, plantations, and other areas of anticipated conflict.

Trail Facilities and Other Considerations

1. Parking is necessary at the trail beginning for the three types of use: pull-through parking for autos with trailers, regular parking for automobiles, and a parking or assembly area for snowmobiles.

2. A suitable area is needed for loading and unloading snowmobiles (ramps) to reduce traffic congestion and provide safety for snowmobilers and pedestrians.

3. A warm up and test area should be provided near the beginning of the trails.

4. Trash receptacles should be provided at the beginning of the trail, at rest areas, or at major trail intersections. Trail users should also be encouraged to carry out what they packed in.

5. Warming shelters and restrooms may be desirable at

the trail beginning and at the half-way point. Take advantage of existing facilities at parks and scenic sites.

6. Snowmobile rental concessions should be privately operated, usually in conjunction with fuel and repair service.

7. Camping facilities may be desirable along extremely long trails. An existing campground could be used as the starting and ending point of the trail.

8. Trails should be routed, where possible, in the vicinity of existing first-aid and emergency facilities, telephones, fuel, and repairs. Directional signs to these areas are recommended and should be noted on all maps and trail information signs.

9. Spur trails to existing towns or service facilities such as restaurants, lodges, or winter sports areas may be considered. Select only spurs that are directly beneficial to snowmobile users and management agencies.

10. Any structures to be built for snowmobile trails such as bridges, buildings, and trail facilities should be aesthetically pleasing.

11. Weather forecasts and trail conditions could be posted at the trail entrance.

12. Local radio stations should be encouraged to broadcast weather forecasts for up-to-date conditions.

13. Snowmobile patrols may be utilized to police trails and aid disabled snowmobiles or injured persons.

Signs and Markers

Standardized signs for snowmobile trails have been recommended and a committee to study this aspect is working toward this goal. Information about sign style and design will soon be made available.

1. The system should be unique in color, size, and

shape. The primary purpose of signing is for the safety and reassurance of trail users. The signing system should be aesthetically acceptable and not offensive in other seasons.

2. An effective signing system should be low to moderate in cost to procure, install, and maintain.

3. Reflectorization is of prime importance for certain types of signs because 25 percent of the snowmobile's use is during hours of reduced light.

4. Minimum yet adequate signing should be the rule. Sufficient signs are needed to ensure user safety, to facilitate enforcement, and to satisfy liability claim requirements.

5. Symbolization should be introduced into the field of snowmobile and recreational signing on a nationwide basis. Symbolization of informational and directional signing permits more rapid comprehension and user response.

6. Consideration should be given to the possibility of incorporating some snowmobile trails into the multipurpose trails system. The possibility of signing for multipurpose trails should not be overlooked.

Snowmobile Sign Design

The signs should follow the standards that the public already knows and should be used wherever the situation exists.

1. Warning signs on highways should be placed at all locations where trails cross roadways. Where possible, crossing should be eliminated by rerouting the trails.

2. Cautionary signs should retain their familiar shape and color for rapid comprehension and to insure maximum safety. Aesthetic qualities must be a secondary con-

sideration in the use of cautionary signing. Highway-type stop and caution signs should be reflectorized for night use.

3. Stop signs should be red octagon with white letters. Caution signs should be yellow diamond with black symbols or letters.

4. The use of symbols is preferred over lettering where they can be utilized because of faster reaction time. Sign size has not been finalized.

5. Trail blazer signs delineate the trail and give assurance that a snowmobile is on it. Its sole purpose is to identify the trail route. To avoid confusion it should not contain information or control or directional features.

6. Adequate directional signing will be needed to supplement the trail blazer at intersections and other key locations. The directional sign should be the same shape and color as the blazer and reflectorized.

Sign Placement

Signs should be placed where trail conditions merit.

1. Caution signs are placed where needed. Stop signs should appear 25 feet from a road crossing and stop-ahead signs 300 feet from the crossing.

2. Informational signs should be conspicuous at the entrance and at major intersections as well as at specific features along the trail.

3. The blazer should be placed often enough to reassure the user. Unless conditions warrant closer or farther sign placement, 250-300 feet is recommended.

4. All signs should be on the right and from 3 to 6 feet from the edge of the trail. Signs should be placed not less than 40 inches above the normal maximum annual snow accumulation.

In *Recreational Industry,* September 1969, the article "Snowmobile Facilities" sums up the problem of adequate facilities:

> The sport of snowmobiling needs to encourage a surge of new and expanded snowmobile facilities to accommodate the increased number of machines and people that will hit the slopes this year and in the years to come. The (snowmobile) industry should strive to establish as many trail locations as possible in areas where usage is now limited. This should be done with the preservation of wildlife and of natural land resources in mind. A sharp eye should be kept out for poor planning of trails which would provoke prohibitive legislation. . . . As new trails are opened up and more people head off for new winter adventures, proper trail markings and development of resort areas will become even more important. Future needs must be envisioned now.

15

Racing

Snowmobile racing is fast becoming a sport of major status in the North American snowbelt region. Races that draw large crowds have an increasingly large purse for winners who achieve firsts in the many aspects of snowmobile racing. Professionalism among drivers is also growing at a rapid rate.

The history of snowmobile racing has yet to determine when and where was the first race. Only one fact is evident; the racing fever struck several areas in the snow belt region about the same time. The first publicity of any nature concerning racing began in 1962, before much interest had arisen in the sport in general. The impact of snowmobile racing has even overflowed into summer when races are held on grass and on indoor tracks.

Although snowmobile racing comprises approximately two percent of the total sport, tourism and increased professional enthusiasm has contributed a tremendous interest. Individuals and teams from Canada and the United

States participate in races all over both countries. If there are any doubts to the rapid growth of this sport, just look around and see the number of new tracks that have been opened since 1965. There are a dozen or so major races held every winter that each attract more than 500 racers. The veteran professional is fast displacing the amateur driver, and manufacturers are becoming more involved in sponsoring drivers and providing equipment. Although the amateur racer remains the backbone, industry has shown that machines with modifications need special competition.

Prizes range from simple trophies in small races to over $30,000 in major events across the United States and Canada. Since 1967 a "pro" racing circuit has been created. The circuit started in Minnesota with professionals participating in races held on flat, oval tracks. The competitors usually had manufacturers sponsor them, but there were also independent teams. As the circuit became more successful races were held in different types of tracks—the oval, the closed, the cross-country—and some found speed could be markedly increased if curves were banked. The Birchwood track in Duluth, Minnesota, was designed for snowmobile racing but fashioned after the Grand Prix road racing track with both right- and left-hand banked turns and a number of straightaways. In Michigan a 500-mile snowmobile race at Sault Ste. Marie patterned itself after the Daytona 500, the object being to achieve high speed and endurance.

Race sanctioning by the United States Snowmobile Association and the Canadian and American Snowmobile Racing Association has added to the acceptability of the sport by setting standards of competition. Areas and tracks would submit their plans for an intended race early in order to become sanctioned.

The most sought after trophy in Canada is the Kawartha Cup, which is a traveling trophy. The race is held in Peterborough, Ontario, in February. Just recently races involving women have added to this attraction.

In small towns the snowmobile purse is small but the excitement of the sport is anything but small. Snowmobile racing is colorful and the array of colors lends excitement to the competitive atmosphere. The amount of money spent by manufacturers on racing is enormous. They not only sponsor drivers but provide equipment, entry fees, transportation, mechanics, trucks, buses, and cars with the various parts and tools. Publicity people are also sent to the race sites by manufacturers with all the extras of a convention, which are used to create interest in the race and in the particular model the manufacturer hopes to sell. In return, the manufacturer obtains important information for research and development of better machines and creates public interest in successful brands. Manufacturers can boast of their machine's capabilities and of the national and international championships their snowmobiles have captured. In a recent survey, one race cost manufacturers from $2,000 to $40,000, but the increased sales did offset the amount of money expended by a fantastic amount in most cases.

In Canada, the Canadian and American Snowmobile Racing Association has attempted to separate the professional driver from the amateur driver. A book of competition rules was patterned after the Sports Car Club of America and registration began in Minnesota. In separating the events, 12 races in the United States and Canada were limited to professional drivers and manufacturer teams. The racetracks had to meet certain standards for safety and spectators, and the sponsor had to follow the organization's established guidelines for the conduct of the race. The response to this procedure has been both good and bad. Those who approve of the racing circuit for professionals feel that the few major professional races would bring more spectators and better press coverage than a larger number. Those against the circuit felt that the Canadian and American Snowmobile Racing Association and the United States Snowmobile Association would become too involved with the racing aspect of snowmobiling and would not give as much service to the non-racing activities that comprise the greatest amount of interest in the sport. A steering committee to study the question was set up for 1971 and the results of their work will be instrumental in the future of the professional racing circuit.

Women in snowmobile racing have not been forgotten, and most races include a Powder Puff as well as a Junior Race. The first idea of these specific races was to relieve tension, but interest in women's and junior's racing has become a major attraction in some areas.

Now that people by the thousands are becoming interested in racing both from the driver's point of view and the spectator's point of view, there are certain aspects of racing that should be understood. Snowmobile racing is still in its infancy—many novice fans and drivers are lured to the various tracks to try their skill. Bombardier Ltd., manufacturer of Ski-Doo and the pioneer producer of the two-passenger snowmobile, has created a guide for prospective snowmobile racers. Below are a few excerpts from this pamphlet that may assist future snowmobile competitors in learning the necessary information about racing.

What, exactly, is a snowmobile race? Surprisingly enough, this question is not as easy to answer as it might seem. Rules and regulations governing the fast-growing sport of snowmobile racing vary from one corner of snow country to the other. And while the idea of getting from one place to another ahead of the next person is a universal concept, snowmobile racers do not necessarily follow the same path.

In general, it can be said that snowmobile races traditionally developed at the regional level, and are the product of local attitudes. Terrain also plays a big factor in determining the type of race that will be held in a given area.

For example, in rural Quebec, where the snowmobile concentration is probably higher than anywhere else in the world, hill climbs are more popular than they are elsewhere. The French Canadians also appreciate the challenge of a fast ½ mile speed oval race track where they can fly over snow at speeds up to 65 mph and around turns that are banked as high as 20 feet.

At the annual Trapper's Festival at the Pas in Northern Manitoba, snowmobiles compete on the same program with dog sled races, tea-boiling contests, snowshoe runs, and flour packing contests. In the latter event, husky trappers carry flour sacks weighing up to 700 pounds on their backs across the snow.

The good trappers who hold forth in Manitoba's rich pulpwood country take a rather utilitarian view of the whole business of racing snowmobiles. A snowmobile is a snowmobile anywhere else, but in Northern Manitoba it is a power toboggan!

Alaska's frozen tundra provides the back drop for one of the most grueling snowmobile racing events yet conceived. The Midnight Sun 600 features a three-day, 600 mile run from Anchorage to Fairbanks in a cross-country spectacular that provides a rugged test for men and machines.

Perhaps the most unusual snowmobile race ever held featured a single racing team of amateur cold country explorers. Theirs was a race against the fickle elements of Arctic weather and was conducted over frozen, shifting ice floes in sub-zero cold. Ralph Plaisted and his team of American and Canadian explorers beat the elements in their dash for the North Pole on Ski Doos, arriving April 19, 1968.

Most snowmobile racing derbies attempt to test the skills of drivers in more than one event. Snowmobiles are designed to do a whole lot more than drive around in circles, and spectators appreciate this point. They also appreciate the fact that the action is often difficult to follow. For this reason, a brief explanation of the types of races and race courses that have developed may prove helpful:

Drag Course: A straightaway sprint for speed over distances up to a quarter-mile. Races are held on either snow or grass, and, in some areas, sophisticated electronic timing devices have been installed to check driver times.

Closed Course: An endless track resembling a sports car road course. In fact, snowmobile races are sometimes held on suitable sports car courses. This type of run generally features hill, valleys, flat areas and turns in both directions. Many drivers favor this type of course for a distance of about five miles because it can offer a good test of driver skills, and because the race can easily be supervised.

Oval or Circular Closed Course: Usually laid out in a bowl shape with banked turns, and resembles the tracks used by midget autos, stock cars and the like. The race is for a specified number of laps, and in some areas is held indoors on artificial snow or dirt.

Obstacle or Slalom Course: Combines tight turns,

banks, jumps and other difficult assignments, but places a premium on speed. It is a relatively short course with each machine racing alone against the clock.

Cross-country Course: As the name implies, a long distance event designed to test both navigational skills and machine and driver performance from one point to another. Cross-country combines the challenges of the obstacle course with long straight stretches and is generally raced against the clock, in groups, on a course varying from 25 to 100 miles or more.

Enduro Course: Either a closed course or an open country course, with the race run over an extended period of time to place a premium on the endurance of driver and machine.

Jumping Course: This is not truly a racing course, but jumping events are normally held in conjunction with snowmobile races. The jumping course normally provides a straightaway approach leading to a 12-foot ramp with a regulation 30-inch rise at the far end. Machines hit this ramp individually and fly into space to land on snow or hay. The winner is determined by the horizontal distance from takeoff to the spot where the rear of machine touches down. At the big meets, it will require a jump approaching 80 feet to win.

Now that the facilities have been explained, the classification of the various machines must be considered. Snowmobiles are divided into various classes, depending upon the cubic centimeter of engine displacement and whether the machine is a stock vehicle (without any manufacturer changes) or a modified one (where the engine has been "souped" up). The reason why there are various classes is to ensure the racer that his competitors have the same mechanical qualities. Below are typical racing classifications as explained by the Bombardier pamphlet.

UNITED STATES SNOWMOBILE ASSOCIATION

STOCK		MODIFIED		POWDER PUFF (stock only)	
Class A	0 to 250 cc	Class I	0 to 295 cc	PP-I	0 to 250 cc
Class B	251 to 295 cc	Class II	296 to 340 cc	PP-II	251 to 295 cc
Class C	296 to 345 cc	Class III	341 to 440 cc	PP-III	296 to 345 cc
Class D	346 to 400 cc	Class IV	441 to 800 cc	PP-IV	346 to 400 cc

JUNIOR (stock only)
J-I   0 to 250 cc
J-II   251 to 295 cc
J-III 296 to 345 cc

CANADIAN SNOWMOBILE ASSOCIATION

Class A	0 to 350 cc	FREE-FOR-ALL CLASS	
Class B	351 to 440 cc	Class I	0 to 440 cc
Class C	441 to 800 cc	Class II	441 to 800 cc

AMERICAN SNOWMOBILE ASSOCIATION

STOCK		MODIFIED	
Class A	0 to 295 cc	Class I	0 to 295 cc
Class B	296 to 345 cc	Class II	296 to 340 cc
Class C	346 to 400 cc	Class III	341 to 440 cc
		Class IV	441 to 800 cc

Modified snowmobiles are so complicated and varied that categorizing them becomes very difficult. The only control over them while racing is determined by the cubic centimeter engine displacement. Souping-up the engine so it becomes a high-powered machine, capable of reaching tremendous speeds and enduring the greatest amount of stress in order to achieve maximum results, is a skill reserved for a select few. If factories modify their machines for competition they train drivers to handle this more powerful model. If the driver makes changes in the manufacturer's specifications he does so with the belief that his skill can improve the speed and maneuverability, testing the highest potential that the engine can offer. The mechanic must not only have a thorough knowledge of the mechanical functioning of the snowmobile in its stock condition, but he must have the ability to know how the changes will affect it as it glides over all types of snow and track conditions.

Many alterations have enabled machines to reach speeds no one ever thought they could reach in their present form. Manufacturers welcome changes in design as they gain valuable data to help them improve on the principles of snowmobile production. Recently, lowering the center of gravity has decreased the snowmobile's tendency to tip over, improved mufflers have led to quieter vehicles, and improved suspension systems have made the vehicles more comfortable. These are only a few changes that have been made to improve snowmobiles. A current trend is to have manufacturers send racing teams to the various races to test the new designs that were created in the factory. Of course if their vehicle won, their publicity would include this added feature in depicting the qualities of their brand.

With such a rapid increase in snowmobiling, control of racing has become a problem. Since racing thus far is held only in the United States and Canada, organizations to control the sport within each country and between the two countries have been created. The basic responsibilities of these organizations concern not only legislation but safety, licensing, sanctioning of events, rules of competition and machine classification, and approval of track layouts with regulations concerning their condition. There are about 20 organizations or associations, the most active being the United States Snowmobile Association, the Western Snowmobile Association, the Canadian Snowmobile Association, the American Snowmobile Association, and the Canadian and American Snowmobile Racing Association.

Keeping track of the various races that are held from November to March is very difficult because of the newness of the sport and the number of organizations controlling its activities. Of course, major snowmobile events are well publicized and attendance grows each season. In some areas television coverage adds to the excitement. In small towns, the enthusiasm may only be local but its value to the total sport cannot be forgotten. Whether a race is large or small there are certain characteristics that are all common.

The racing spectator comes in three varieties. First is the curiosity seeker who has cultivated an interest through his personal recreational snowmobiling and wants to see a little more excitement than usual. Next comes the Sunday snowmobile spectator, who just can't wait until the Sunday finals so he can be there for the well-publicized major event. The third type is the racing bug who has the time and money and who travels here and there wherever the action is, just to see the big names and the new records set. Small-town races have little appeal to this person; he wants front row center at the big ones.

In general all spectators have one problem: how to keep warm while watching the race. They come dressed in all kinds of attire in hopes that they will outlast the races. Again, the Snowmobile Racing Primer suggests the following tips on how to weep warm in the stands.

1. Be sure your feet are well protected in nylon top rubber bottom boots with a warm inner liner.

2. Cover your hands with mitts or gloves.

3. Make sure your cap or toque offers adequate protection for the ears.

4. Thermal underwear will be necessary when the thermometer drops, particularly if there is a strong wind.

When the race begins the smaller machines in the first classifications begin early in the day. As the race continues, the heavier, more powerful machines, which add excitement to the race, enter the picture. The track or course becomes less desirable with use and the big machines, traveling at a high rate of speed, take a great deal of punishment. One race rapidly follows the other, giving the spectator little time to catch his breath or lose interest, except in the endurance-type races that go on for long periods of time. A snowmobile race usually continues for two or three days, with the first day centering its activities toward the elimination of inadequate contestants. In major races, hundreds of entries competing for only a few prizes must be narrowed down to the best few. The races are not only divided into classes but also into heats, and usually the first three winners in each heat are allowed to continue. In this way a driver who has come in second or third still has a chance to win the final event, which is often held on a separate day, in most cases on Sunday. From the elimination heats the best machines have been selected for each event. The finals are also held separately so the track can be prepared and in the best condition.

In some races, the tension mounts so rapidly that other events—junior and women events, derbies of countless varieties, cross country races, and slalom contests—are scheduled to relieve spectator stress.

As in auto racing, the flags are very important to the contestants as well as to the spectator. Flagmen keep the race organized and keep the spectators aware of what is going on. There are various methods of starting races with flags, all of which depend on the type of race, the two most frequent being the standing start and the flying start. In the standing start the snowmobiles line up and on a given signal from the starter the race begins. Snowmobiles lap the oval track in predetermined starting positions on the flying start. When all is well the starter signals by waving a green flag. Flags have specific colors that tell contestants what to do. The green flag begins the race on an oval track and is displayed by the starter throughout the race as long as everything is all right. If a problem occurs, such as an accident, the starter displays a yellow flag, which means all vehicles must decelerate. Drivers must watch the starter for further signals. On cross country courses, the yellow flag also indicates potential danger. At any time during a race if a red flag is shown it means that a major problem has been created and all vehicles must stop immediately.

A white flag will be displayed by the starter indicating the final lap on an oval course. Anytime a black flag is displayed to a specific driver, he must report to his pit area. The flag warning system is the greatest safety feature of any race and flagmen are placed strategically around the track or course. Flagmen are also considered officials and have the power to disqualify drivers for deviating from the rules and regulations.

Because of man's love for speed and excitement and his desire for competition, snowmobile racing provides a means to satisfy this need. Below are a few competitive events that have contributed to the fast growth of snow mobile racing.

Hodag Cross-Country Marathon—Rhinelander, Wisconsin

World Championship Snowmobile Race—Eagle River, Wisconsin

Kawartha International—Peterborough, Ontario

Boubon Cup Championship—Boonville, New York

West Yellowstone Roundup—West Yellowstone, Montana

King Castle Grand Prix—Lake Tahoe, Nevada

Marienvill Races—Marienville, Pennsylvania

Canadian Championship—Beausejour, Winnipeg, Canada

Trappers' Festival—Pas, Manitoba

Western Canadian Championship—Vernon, British Columbia

Quebec City Winter Carnival—Quebec, Canada

Oval Championships—Butte, Montana

Paul Bunyan Classic—Brainerd, Minnesota

Munising Cross Country—Munising, Michigan

New Hampshire Grand Prix—Bryar Motor Sport Park, New Hampshire

Alaska 600—Anchorage, Alaska

St. Paul Winter Carnival 500—Winnipeg, Minnesota

Sault Ste. Marie International 500—Sault Ste. Marie, Michigan

Central Division USSA Championship—Birchwood, Duluth, Minnesota

State Dominion Snowmobile Rally—Thief River Falls, Minnesota

These are just a few of the more highly publicized races eld throughout the United States and Canada. Information concerning races in your area can be obtained by writing to any of the associations listed in the Appendix or from such magazines as the *Sno-Mobile Times,* Minneapolis, Minnesota, or the *Michigan Snowmobiler* in Eaton Rapids, Michigan.

16

Safety and Common Hazards

The mobility of the snowmobile enables it to travel great distances and over rugged terrain allowing the rider enjoyment, adventures, thrills, and excitement. By 1972 it is estimated over two million people will own snowmobiles, with 90 percent of them using their vehicle for a various number of recreational activities.

With an increasing number of people participating in the sport of snowmobiling comes an increase in the number of hazards. A safety campaign to keep the sport free from death and injury has been instigated by a number of manufacturers and organizations. The average citizen does not realize how important such a program is until he is directly involved in an accident. Manufacturers are constantly producing better machines with greater safety features. With these improvements comes a fusing of many interdependent forces working for safer snowmobiling conditions.

Within the safety movement, education serves as a

directional signal, indicating which way the sport will go
Few snowmobile accidents can be attributed to chance
and most result from inadequate knowledge of the rules.
Many of the safety programs in existence deal with these
three aspects as well as making machines and facilities
safer.

Sites for snowmobile activities are almost endless. The
snowmobiler must first become aware of the hazards that
exist in the areas he wishes to use, and he must learn the
simple rules that allow him to participate in the sport
safely. Then, when the snowmobiler understands the hazards and compensates for the dangers over which he has
no control, he develops attitudes that will carry him
through without adverse experiences.

Safe preparation first begins on a personal basis. Here
are ten rules each snowmobiler should follow:

1. Be sure you are physically able to participate; have
a physical if necessary and never go snowmobiling when
you are ill or have an injury.

2. Never drive the snowmobile under mental anguish;
you may hurt yourself and others as the result of an
unthinking act.

3. Never snowmobile under the influence of alcohol
or drugs.

4. Know basic first aid and where to send for help if
the need arises.

5. Use the snowmobile only for the purpose for which
it was intended.

6. Keep your equipment in its proper working order
and possess all basic equipment.

7. Know your capabilities, use mature judgment, and
act within these limits.

8. Learn all about snow conditions and how to cope with or remove hazards that might occur in the wilderness.

9. Learn the laws of your state and of the area in which you will be; follow them religiously.

10. Have a safe attitude and do nothing to create hazards for other snowmobilers.

It is difficult to compare the dangers of snowmobiling to other recreational activities. In relation to other sports, the percentage of injuries and deaths is low. The National Safety Council estimates that the majority of accidents and deaths were unnecessary. Although only two percent of snowmobilers engage in racing activities and the other 98 percent participate in recreational snowmobiling, 75 percent of accidents happened to recreational snowmobilers. All reported deaths up to January 1970 have occurred in non-racing activities.

The snowmobile itself is not dangerous; it only becomes dangerous by unsafe use. The actual risk a snowmobiler takes when he sets out on a cruise in the frigid wilderness is no greater than participating in one of the many other pastimes, or for that matter, even driving the car to the corner store. Experience makes a person more cautious, and for this reason, nothing more than common sense and mature understanding are needed to make the sport enjoyable. If a beginner snowmobiler expresses a willingness to learn and has mature judgment to begin with, he will probably become experienced with very little pain. To begin with, the snowmobiler must be skilled with hand as well as mind. If something unexpected should happen on the trail, it is important to eliminate the hazard quickly and with as little emotion as possible.

A casual interest in snowmobiling is not enough prerequisite for planning a trip of any length. The best, easiest, and safest methods must be learned, and although most tasks can be learned easily, only those persons really interested in being a safe snowmobiler should pursue the sport. The snowmobiler must possess the knowledge of out-of-door living, navigation, and mechanics of the machine.

Any snowmobile trip carries with it a set of principles that are considered calculated risks. How the individual handles these risks depends on knowledge as well as experience, Many are obvious, but the individual must be prepared for the unexpected. Generally, in calculating risks certain facts must be considered. First is skill. The skilled snowmobiler operates his vehicle with great efficiency and by doing so increases the safety factor. Second is emotion. How an individual handles his emotions may mean the difference between having an accident or not. Third is knowledge. Knowing the rules of safety decreases risks, but practicing what is known is even more important. Last is organization. The ability to organize activities into meaningful and acceptable behavior will eventually lead to a low accident ratio. This principle is dependent upon adequate leadership, proper administration, safe equipment, driver skill, and control of environmental conditions.

In attempting to understand the hazards of snowmobiling, one must consider the nature of the activities involved, the equipment (including all accessories) , the responsibility for control, the facilities and the classification of the various participants. In making the sport safe, all unnecessary hazards must be determined and removed. This may be done by simply improving a mechanical feature on the snowmobile or a physical feature of a trail. It may also be accomplished by eliminating misinformation about a particular snowmobile maneuver. Even though every attempt will be made to eliminate unnecessary hazards not every one could be removed; they might only be controlled. For example, racing is obviously more dangerous than snow cruising, but the driver who understands the hazards will develop skills to overcome them and keep danger to a minimum. It is also important to be constantly aware that new hazards arise and try hard not to create added problems. Since snowmobiling is so new, it is important that the first steps in its organization emphasize safety.

A snowmobile safety code has been created by several snowmobile organizations:

When planning extended trips, I will prepare a route plan with an estimated time of return. I will give this information to a responsible person. When traveling on State or Federally owned lands, I will check in and check out with the park officials or ranger station.

When making extended trips, I will carry emergency equipment (snowshoes or skis, flares, tow line, waterproof matches, emergency food supply, extra fuel, compass and map). I will avoid traveling alone in remote areas.

I will not cross or travel on frozen lakes and streams until the ice is thick enough to support the weight of my snowmobile and passengers. When traveling in new areas, I will seek advice on ice conditions.

I will keep myself physically fit for winter sports.

I will always carry a first aid kit.

I will wear proper winter clothing and protective glasses or goggles.

I will know the weather forecast. When the weather turns bad, I will turn back.

I will keep my snowmobile in good operating condition.

I will always carry a tool kit.

I will stay on marked trails or marked roads open to snowmobiles. I will avoid cross-country travel unless specifically authorized.

I will use my snowmobile only for transportation when hunting. My rifle will be encased whenever I am aboard my snowmobile if local regulations allow encased rifles aboard snowmobiles.

Bombardier, Ltd., manufacturer of Ski-Doo, with the assistance of the National Safety Council in Chicago, Illinois, has created a booklet on the do's and don'ts of snowmobiling. Below are the highlights from this booklet:

Do's

1. Do obtain operating instructions.
2. Do position is sitting down with both feet inside the cab or on the boards but not locked into the foot rests.
3. A do for bumpy terrain is to place one knee on the seat for better balance, and for "side hilling" it's better to lean into the hill from this position.
4. Lengthen throttle cable when teaching children. Warn against speed, overconfidence and carelessness. Never let children snowmobile alone. Know your child's capabilities and shortcomings. Be certain he knows the rules and teach for safe operation. Common sense, courtesy and respect for the vehicle are fundamental.
5. Always play safe with children aboard. Exert extra care. Avoid treacherous sidehills and broken terrain. See that the child firmly grips the handles and is properly seated with feet parallel on the boards. Check this frequently.
6. Do use a tow-bar when pulling a trailer of any sort.
7. Do check lights before starting to snowmobile at night. Avoid river and lake crossings and don't break new trails.
8. Properly secure your snowmobile to its trailer and

protect it with a bright cover. Check the trailer hitch and lights before leaving and make sure all equipment is securely fastened to the trailer.

9. Come to a complete stop before crossing any street or highway. Cross only at 90 degree angles to the roadway and remember that traffic always has the right of way. Know the local regulations. Have one person watch for traffic while the other person crosses with the snowmobile.

10. Dress warmly.

11. The trailer should carry snowshoes for each person, extra fuel, emergency rations, a first aid kit, flares, a knife, and waterproof matches on all long trips.

12. Travel with extreme caution in unknown areas, follow marked trails.

13. The same supplies needed on safaris are needed for an overnight camping adventure. Leave the campsite clean.

Don'ts

1. Don't tail-gate. Maintain a "stoppable" speed.

2. Don't cut across another's right of way. Watch for the other guy.

3. Don't attempt to cross ice before checking its thickness.

4. Never use a railroad right of way and cross only at a 90 degree angle. Shut off your machine before crossing so you can hear an approaching train.

5. Don't be a show off.

6. Don't cut fences or trample shrubs. Get permission to use private property.

7. Don't leave your key in the ignition.

8. Snowmobile only in areas provided for that purpose.

9. Check your throttle before you start out. If it should stick—*Don't Panic*—just turn off the ignition key.

10. If the back becomes stuck in deep snow do not put your hands or feet near the track while it is driving, in attempting to free your machine. Lift out the back end

and drive it out while kneeling with one leg on the seat and pushing off with your free leg. You may also push the machine out by the handlebars while standing next to it and squeezing the throttle lightly.

Teaching children to snowmobile will help end frequent violations of snowmobile regulations and make the sport safer. Youths are not aware of the laws that govern the sport and must be taught by adults. In East Jordan, Michigan, the East Jordan Snowmobilers Inc. club organized a study program for Michigan children. The program attracted over 100 boys and girls from 6 to 16. These children attended two night sessions of demonstrations and discussions and participated in an afternoon safari the next day where their information was tested. A local police officer outlined the laws, a conservation officer explained snowmobile use on public owned property, experienced drivers showed how to make repairs on the trail, and a Red Cross instructor demonstrated emergency treatment. On the trail the adult leaders supervised the children in a two-hour trip, which included a midway cook-out. The Michigan 4-H Youth Program, the Minnesota Safety Training Program, and the International Snowmobile Industry Association also have similar programs. Communities all over the snow-belt region are finding the time spent in such instruction is well worth it and are incorporating such training programs into their yearly activities. The International Snowmobile Industry Association also has a $5000 contribution program to help promote safety programs in addition to providing other safety services and equipment.

It is without question that the greatest criticism of snowmobiling has been caused by careless drivers. These egotistical people have no respect for the rights of others and have left their mark on hundreds of miles of snowmobile trails. On the other hand, the papers are filled with the good and safe things snowmobilers have done. In Albany, New York, 65 snowmobiles driven by volunteers operated emergency runs during a state of emergency. In Pennsylvania, state troopers brought food and fuel to families marooned on snow drifts via snowmobile. In Michigan, snowmobiles—manned by police, firemen, and local organizations of volunteers—transported medicine, doctors, and patients to and from hospitals during an emergency in 1967.

In 1969 the National Safety Council, in a review of reported snowmobile accidents, reported a loss of 39 lives due to snowmobile accidents. The accidents were classified into five areas: drowning, collision with other vehicles, collision with fixed objects, collision with trains, and other accidents. To add to their report the Province of Quebec Safety League reported 24 deaths and 700 injuries, while the Ontario Safety League reported 29 deaths and 300 nonfatal injuries.[4] Dr. Richard W. McLay presented to the 1969 International Snowmobile Conference a report of a snowmobile accident study in Vermont. The study showed 63 reported cases separated into six categories: collision with another vehicle or object, people struck down by a snowmobile, people thrown during maneuvers, people injured in jumps, people injured by barbed wires or chains, and minor injuries. The report continued to list nine special hazards that might present problems to snowmobile operation:[5]

Jumps. The most prevalent cause of broken backs was found to be jumping the vehicle.

4 Fleming, John P. *Proceedings of the International Snowmobile Conference.* Albany, New York, May 1969, p. 24.
5 McLay, Dr. Richard W. *Proceedings of the International Snowmobile Conference.* Albany, New York, May 1969, p. 28.

Lack of Experience. Many of the interviewed revealed that injuries occurred soon after the family acquired the snowmobile.

Poor Visibility. Several accidents were caused when the operators overdrove their headlights and were unable to stop or to avoid hitting something.

Speed. Many accidents could have been avoided if the operators had reduced speed in line with the snow and weather conditions.

Alcohol. A few people admitted having a couple of drinks before demonstrating their driving skills for friends.

Barbed Wire. The hazard is, of course, related to speed and lack of visibility.

Climbing Over Banks. Several accidents occurred when the operators attempted to climb a steep bank such as at a roadside.

Equipment Not in Repair. One case involved a man operating the machine with the throttle wire wrapped around his finger.

Thin Ice. Several drownings have occurred in Lake Champlain when snowmobiles broke through the ice.

Accident prevention can only be effective if the forces that cause accidents are studied. To achieve this, an adequate accident reporting system should be created where there is uniformity in reporting procedures.

In the proceedings of the International Snowmobile Conference, three factors must be considered when discussing snowmobile safety: human factors, machine considerations, and environmental factors. In discussing human factors, Dr. Henry Kao believes certain rules must be established to minimize this factor:

1. Limit the horsepower
2. Develop a registration system
3. Develop educational guidelines for safety

4. Include safety packages as part of vehicle sales
5. Apply anthropometric data in designing snowmobiles
6. Recommend the sale of safety helmets as standard equipment
7. Recommend colors of high environmental contrast
8. Use heavy padding on the instrument panel
9. Develop a snowmobile safety patrol system
10. Improve present snowmobile lighting systems

Richard W. McLay explains that there are six factors concerning areas where machine improvement and operation are necessary:

1. Visibility
2. Maintenance
3. Eliminate jumping on the advertising
4. Building up seats
5. Towing Sleds
6. Noise

Lastly, unsafe environmental factors concerned:
1. Tree Lines
2. Wide open areas
3. Weather
4. Windchill
5. Carbon monoxide and gasoline explosions
6. Litter
7. Unified educational program

For further information on snowmobile safety, consult the following publications:

Fun Guide to
Snowmobiling
Public Relations Dept.
Johnson Motors
Waukegan, Illinois

Polaris Safety Pamphlet
Polaris, Inc.
Roseau, Minnesota

*Owner's Safety
  Handbook*
Arctic Enterprises, Inc.
Thief River Falls, Minn.

*Minnesota Snowmobile
  Safety*
Conservation Department
St. Paul, Minnesota

*Play Safe for More
  Winter Fun*
Bombardier Ltd.
Valcourt, Quebec,
  Canada

Safe Snowmobile Operation
Conservation Dept. Div. of
  Lands and Forests
Albany, New York

To encourage safe snowmobiling, Polaris, Inc. of Roseau, Minnesota, has created a colorful emblem and has distributed it to their local dealers to be given to people who complete a snowmobile safety test. A gimmick for safety, yes, but any publicity to encourage safe behavior is well worth the effect.

Safety tips geared to give basic information have been compiled by many sources. A summary of this information is given here.

1. Digest your snowmobile's factory manual.

2. Test your snowmobile frequently and become familiar with all working parts.

3. Always check the throttle before starting the engine.

4. Although a free-running track is necessary for proper snowmobile operation, never have someone lift the back while the track is running. Use the warm-up stand or have two people support the machine.

5. Start slowly and become familiar with proper riding positions.

6. Learn how to lean on various degrees of turns and find out how quick you must change weight on all changes in direction.

7. Learn how to drive with one knee on the seat when side-hilling.

8. By law and common sense, never allow an individual under 12 to drive alone.

9. Provide adequate training for all youths.

10. Know and practice gradual acceleration and avoid fast starts from a dead stop.

11. When driving at night use extra caution, check your lighting system, and carry extra bulbs. Never travel on ice at night.

12. Never travel alone at night.

13. Stay on trails at night and never trail blaze in the dusk or dark.

14. Check all trailers, sleds, or toboggan hitches and never use wire or old rope to secure these accessories.

15. A rigid tow bar is recommended and important to the stability of any pulled accessory.

16. Avoid rear-end collisions by keeping a safe distance between snowmobiles.

17. Approach snowmobile intersections slowly. If there is a stop sign don't just slow down—stop.

18. Be sure the trail is wide enough for snowmobile passing and never pass while going uphill.

19. Know your snow conditions and check weather forecasts frequently.

20. Wear sunglasses to avoid excess glare.

21. Never wear sunglasses at night.

22. On glare ice, slow down as the back end may decide to get ahead of the front end causing a serious spin or spill.

23. When traveling on lakes that have patches of snow and ice, extra care is needed to avoid spins or spills. Go slow.

24. Stay away from slush on lakes. If you become in-

volved in slush, keep going. Once you stop you may not be able to get going again.

25. Check your gas gauge often and always have gas to spare when you start your return trip.

26. Never pour oil in the gas tank; it does not mix well. It must be mixed thoroughly with gas in a can or it will affect the engine's operation.

27. Leave word of your travels, even for a short trip.

28. Have more equipment than you think you will need, even on an afternoon cruise, you may be surprised.

29. Always carry a tool kit, a first aid kit, and a survival kit.

30. Carry an extra drive belt.

The last area that should be considered is the procedure you should follow if an accident of personal injury or property damage has occurred.

1. Stop at once. If the snowmobiles can be pulled to one side of the road or trail, do so. This is especially true on the up hill. Turn off the ignition and do not smoke near the accident.

2. Avoid making any rash statement, and above all do not argue. Leave the blame for the accident for police and insurance companies to decide for you.

3. Get help for the injured. Avoid doing further damage by moving the injured unless their position is unsafe and you have been trained to move an injured person. Remember to handle injured parts with care. If you are qualified, administer first aid. It also helps to obtain the injured person's permission in the presence of a witness.

4. If the accident has caused injury to anyone or property damage over $50, in most states you must report it to the proper officials.

5. If possible, keep a record of all information. Name of the reporting officer and his badge and post number, all the circumstances (date, hour, location, visibility, weather), and any other existing conditions. If anyone is taken to the hospital, get the name and address of the hospital and the person.

6. The only information you are required by law to give to police is your name and address. If you are questioned inform the officer you would like to consult your attorney before answering. This information may be used against you in a criminal or civil suit.

7. Even if you were at fault do not admit anything at the scene. Sometimes anxiety may distort the way things seem to you and you may be sorry afterwards.

8. Never sign anything until you have consulted a lawyer or your insurance company.

9. Do not say you are not injured, as only a physician can determine your physical condition and something might occur later.

17

When You Are Lost

Generally it is hard to foresee getting lost, especially if you know the area in which you are traveling or someone with you is familiar with it. Realistically, however, there are times when the unexpected happens, even when all logic does not support the possibility. The smart thing to do when traveling in the winter wilderness is to be prepared by learning how to survive in cold climates. Even the most minor emergency may pose a serious problem as it usually occurs in remote inaccessible locations.

Be Prepared

On short snowmobile trips you probably will not have food, although it is a good idea to always carry some nonperishable energy-producing food on the snowmobile. The two essentials necessary for survival (beside food) are warmth and shelter. To begin with, if you are dressed properly for snowmobiling at all times, your personal warmth will not pose as much a problem as it would if you did not have appropriate attire for the conditions. Your biggest task if you anticipate any extended stay in the wilderness is to find some kind of shelter. After your shelter is established, a fire will be your only other way to keep warm. Since we have stressed having a survival kit on the snowmobile at all times, the following items are basic:

1. Plastic poncho or tarpaulin
2. Non-perishable high-energy food
3. Knife
4. Hand axe
5. Toilet tissue
6. Rope
7. Magnifying glass
8. Colored chalk
9. Maps
10. Waterproof matches
11. A few feet of aluminum foil
12. One leakproof can
13. Compass
14. Flares
15. Water-purifying tablets
16. Shovel

Organize Your Activities

The attitude you take will help direct your response to the situation at hand. If you panic and run hysterically, you may lose your life. Your first job is to get into the right frame of mind. At least tell yourself there are people who have survived extended periods of time in winter climates and you can too. Sit down, think through your problem calmly, organize your thoughts, and come up with a course of action with alternatives. Even if you are alone, don't look at it from that point of view, as there is usually someone, somewhere who will realize your absence.

In organizing your thoughts, think about the trail; even write down anything you can remember about it and try to reconstruct your travels. Make notes of any recognizable landmarks. With a pencil or a stick draw a map on paper or in the snow showing where you started, where you were heading, and how much time had elapsed. Estimate your average speed to determine about how far away you are. For instance, if you were traveling approximately 15 miles an hour for one hour and a half you are probably from 22 to 25 miles from your point of departure.

After thinking about your situation your next step is to decide whether to stay where you are or try to find a route out. Take into consideration weather conditions, time of day, your personal stamina and physical condition, what equipment you have, how much gas you have, who knows your scheduled route, and how cold you are. Take time to make this decision and be thoroughly rested before you actually decide what to do. If you decide to stay where you are, it may mean an overnight campout, so keep this in mind.

In making any kind of plans, keep in mind alternatives to these plans. In most cases they may be very few, in other cases you may find a number of choices. For instance you may plan on staying where you are because you have left a plan of your trip and the weather is not cold or snowy, and your gas is low. If you decide to find a way out and have constructed a map, by heading in one direction you may eventually find help, if you and your gas hold out that is.

When trying to find your way out by traveling in a straight line, it is wise to select a target destination that you can see and start traveling toward it. It might be wise to leave marks on trees with colored chalk, as it may snow and cover up your tracks. When you arrive at your target, choose a new target and push ahead. If the terrain is rugged you may have to travel around obstacles. Try to travel so you will not lose visual sight of your destination. If you do, make 90 degree turns if possible. If you are fortunate enough to come across a fire lane, a power or phone line, or even a logging road, keep your eye out for other snowmobile tracks or footprints as they may lead to safety, especially if the track is fresh. Never travel at night as the increase in danger is as great as the possibility of traveling around in a circle.

You may determine direction without a compass. One way is to locate the north by looking for the north star at night. Once you have found the big dipper, the north star is two stars from the front edge of the cup upward. During the day, know that the sun travels east to west. By placing a stick in the snow, you can determine north by the shadow. The stick may also give you the relative time by the position of the shadow. If you have a compass, the face of the compass is marked with the directions of north, east, south, west and 360 degree markers. East is at 90, south 180, west is 270 and north is both 360 and 0. The compass needle will always point toward magnetic north and not the earth's true polar north. The difference between these two points is called the declination or the variation. When you want to travel true north you must use the polar north. To find true north you must make an adjustment by adding westerly declination and taking away the eastern declination. After determining which direction you want to travel, hold the compass in the direction you want to go. Wait for the needle to stop before setting the sighting line, if the compass has one. For a good explanation of compass reading consult Robert S. Owendoff's book, *Better Ways of Pathfinding*, published by Stackpole Books in Harrisburg, Pennsylvania, in 1964.

After you have determined the direction in which you want to travel, select a target and start moving toward your goal. Don't forget to look back occasionally to see if you can find the last landmark you were at. It is also a good policy to note each compass reading on your watch— if you have one—so you will know how long it took you to travel between targets.

Traveling in a circle can be a hazard, but if it is done on purpose it is a very effective method. First you must select a familiar target, then pick one direction and walk straight away from the center point. Mark this new target with chalk, one mark on either side. Repeat this movement of changing targets.

If you are fortunate enough to have a map of the area you are traveling in, most maps give such information as distances between markers, names of ranges, townships and sections, names of trails, roads, streams, peaks, and parks. When using the map try to name one of the symbols on the map, and then determine north and plot your course. On some maps there is information about townships, sections, and acres. It is important to know that a township is an area six miles by six miles, a section is one mile square, and an acre is 660 feet on a side.

If you decide not to try to find a way out of your situation, for one of the many reasons suggested, your first task will be to find shelter. After the shelter is prepared, gather wood to build a fire and make arrangements for melting snow for water and preparing a meal of some kind. It is wise to make some kind of meal before dark and then keep something hot to drink on the fire as night sets in.

Shelters can be made by throwing a tarp over the snowmobile and packing snow around the bottom. The tarpaulin may be made into a lean-to or, if the snow is deep, a shelter could be made by carving a snow cave. After the shelter has been created, wood must be gathered for the fire. Try to have enough to last through the night. Fires also aid in communicating your position to searchers. After the fire is built the meal should be started. Remember to keep stirring snow or it will scorch and taste terrible. Do not eat all your food at one meal; it may be a longer stay than you anticipated. Refer to the chapter on camping for more information.

When the next day arrives, study the new situation. By now your delay will have caused searching parties to be sent out and in most cases there is a good chance you will be found. Again, re-evaluate your position and make another decision to stay put or to attempt to travel on.

A Special Problem

Each year human lives are lost because a snowmobiler and his vehicle have gone through thin ice. Before we leave this section, here are some points to remember if you happen to go through the ice. If the machine is moving when it breaks through it will start going down front end first. If the vehicle has stopped in most cases the back end will submerge first. The snowmobile will float momentarily because of hydrostatic pressure. Once you are in the water, you will not be able to get off the machine. Take a deep breath and ride the snowmobile down until you can stand on it or tread water. Once you are in control, stretch both arms out on the ice and kick vigorously. It is important to keep your body moving in the water as the coldness soon makes the muscles inoperable. Once out find fresh snow and roll in it. The snow absorbs much of the water. If you have to help someone else out of the icy water don't get close to the opening. Again, lay spread eagle on the ice and use a stick or piece of clothing to reach the person. Once you are out you must find shelter immediately. If you must travel any length to reach help, once you start do not stop no matter how miserable you feel. If no help is available you may use this alternative. Build a fire and take off as much clothing as you can spare. While you are standing next to the fire the clothing you have taken off should be placed on ice away from the heat. The clothes will freeze. In about a half hour, take off the remaining clothes and put on the frozen clothes. You will have to crack off the ice by slapping the frozen clothes against a hard object. The moisture is removed by quick freezing and the fire will dry the clothes quickly.

Snowmobiling is a family affair. (Courtesy Johnson Motors)

Always drive in control and never too close to winter cottages. (Courtesy Rupp Industries)

Hang it out, man. Hang it out. (Courtesy *Sno-mobile Times*)

Snowmobile racing accounts for only two percent of all injuries. (Courtesy *Sno-mobile Times*)

"Wipe out" on the way. (Courtesy *Sno-mobile Times*)

An internal combustion engine of a snowmobile. (Courtesy Rupp Industries)

Trailers help to make snowmobiling outings more enjoyable for the family. (Courtesy Johnson Motors)

Always prepare a route plan in duplicate and carry a map of the area where you will be traveling. (Courtesy Johnson Motors)

New in snowmobiling footwear are these eye-appealing snowmobile boots with ankle pads and a removable felt liner. (Courtesy Ski-Doo Sports)

Wearing the latest in snowmobiling and après snowmobiling apparel, these couples enjoy the fun of a winter cookout. Host and hostess are attired in versatile two-piece wool knit suits in solid tones with colorful shoulder and leg stripes. Their snowmobiling friends are wearing one-piece nylon suits, easily unzipped for comfort in varying weather. Apparel by Ski-Doo Sports, Ltd.

Riding the range on horsepower is a common winter sight these days. Whether for ranch chores or high-spirited fun, the snowmobile gives dependable and fast transportation over any snow conditions. (Courtesy Ski-Doo Sports)

For thrill-a-minute action, there's nothing like taking snow-
mobiles into the wide open spaces and opening them up.
These two snowmobilers enjoy a friendly test of machines.
(Courtesy Ski-Doo Sports)

One of the reasons snowmobiling has become the fastest
growing winter sport in North America is the ease of trailer-
ing a machine to the snow, even to the lake cottage as you
would a boat in summer. Many snowmobile dealers sell
special trailers for transporting one or two snowmobiles, as
well as protective covers that help keep a machine looking
like new for years. (Courtesy Ski-Doo Sports)

Frolicking on snowmobiles is most fun in a group. (Courtesy
Ski-Doo Sports)

Like to camp? Then don't put your gear away just because it's snowy winter. These two winter adventurers have easily reached a favorite summer spot even though it's covered with a foot of snow. (Courtesy Ski-Doo Sports)

Winter group safaris by snowmobile into national parks and other scenic winter areas are becoming increasingly popular with outdoor enthusiasts. In fact, many are switching their vacation allegiance from sunny southern beaches to the snow country of the North and West. (Courtesy Ski-Doo Sports)

Snowmobilers and skier get together for a bit of skijoring, a winter sport that lets you ski without a mountain. This snowmobile has enough power to easily pull our friends on skis. Someone should always sit on the snowmobile facing the skier, just like the accepted water skiing safety principle. (Courtesy Ski-Doo Sports)

Sportsmen who ice-fish or hunt in winter weather have found snowmobiles handy for getting to once unreachable fishing spots.

Warmth and safety are the special features of these snow-mobiling caps. The attractive and colorful styling hides a protective inner lining of impact-absorbing cork and foam. The special chin strap holds the cap in place during the most rugged snowmobile action. (Courtesy Ski-Doo Sports)

A winter safari can be great fun if you're well prepared. Extra food, gas, blankets, snowshoes and a reliable snowmobile insure a happy trip and a safe return. (Courtesy Alouette Featherweight Corporation)

Camping was once a sport reserved for summer and fall, but the snowmobile has helped make it a winter sport as well. (Courtesy Alouette Featherweight Corporation)

Snowmobiling provides great fun for the whole family. (Courtesy Sno-Jet)

18

First Aid

On a cold but beautiful December day, a girl named Michelle was given permission by her parents to drive the family snowmobile around the area behind the house. It was Saturday, and Michelle rejoiced that she would not have to go to her sixth-grade class that day and could spend the afternoon riding the new snowmobile. Taking a few precautions, Michelle's dad checked the vehicle over and found it in good working condition. He then gave his daughter the keys and reminded her not to leave the family property. Happily Michelle mounted the snowmobile and off she went. Seeing no problem her dad went inside to do a few chores. After a few minutes he looked out the window to see how she was doing, and as he watched the snowmobile suddenly jerked, throwing Michelle forward and allowing the vehicle to travel over her body. Upon witnessing the tragedy, he ran out of the house to find that the scarf that Michelle was wearing had gotten caught in the working parts of the machine and had pulled her off into its path. Michelle suffered a skull fracture but was very fortunate and survived.

During the same winter in a far northern wilderness, two men riding at night, not knowing the thickness of the ice, proceeded to travel across a small lake. The moon was bright and the snow on the ice was very thick. It was ten degrees above zero and only a few cottages could be seen across the silvery white lake. After traveling a few minutes on the ice the driver had the feeling that the ice ahead might not be solid enough so he stopped the snowmobile in order to assess the situation. Within moments after the snowmobile stopped, the ice beneath gave way, dropping the vehicle and its riders into the cold churning water. Fortunately the men did not panic and were able to get out of the water only to face another grave problem: they were at least three or four miles from their winter cottage. Knowing from their first aid training that since they had no matches and were soaking wet, in order to survive they must obtain shelter. Determining the direction both men started running. At one point, in a state of exhaustion, one of the men wanted to stop, but the other knew that if they did they might not ever start again, so on they pushed. It seemed like hours had passed as they ran through the deep forest snow, when suddenly a dim light appeared. Immediately they headed toward it and found a trailer with an elderly couple who drove them to their cottage. Fortunately the men suffered no physical injury, but the memory of what could have happened haunts them to this day.

These are just two examples of the hazards that could result in injury or death and two reasons why knowledge of first aid is necessary for everyone who is going to participate in snowmobiling.

This chapter on first aid is a straight forward discussion of the common problems that the snowmobiler may become faced with. It is highly recommended that the American Red Cross first aid course be taken for more detailed information. However, a study of common difficulties that a snowmobiler might encounter is discussed in relation to the winter conditions associated with the sport.

It is felt by many safety officials that in an emergency situation man is his own worst enemy, and that through ignorance, carelessness, thoughtlessness, and selfishness he creates his own difficulties. The ability to overcome these problems directly relates to knowledge, skill, and the use of these factors in meeting the problems.

Important also in the prevention of emergencies is the ability to recognize situations that might cause difficulties and to avoid any action that might place an individual or group into a precarious situation.

Safety slogans provide warnings that familiarize people with possible dangers. Any organized safety program attempts to achieve the following goals:

1. To develop knowledge, proper attitudes, and the use of safety skills.

2. To make people aware of the difference between recklessness and adventure.

3. To accept personal responsibility in the prevention of accidents.

4. To protect persons, property, and nature from injury or damage.

An important part of goal one is to encourage all persons to become familiar with the essentials of first aid. Briefly, this chapter deals with the basics of first aid that all snowmobilers should know before participating in the sport. It is quite obvious that when a serious situation arises the snowmobiler must have this knowledge readily available.

When snowmobiling first began, serious and freakish

accidents were considered rare, but now they are common. In 1965 there were 50 accidents per 200,000 vehicles, while in 1969 there were 600 for every 40,000. The fatality rate of snowmobiling has risen in 1970 to the highest rate for any recreational sport. Although snowmobile manufacturers have begun several campaigns to abort the rapidly growing death rate, accidents still claim many lives every year. In 1972 it is estimated that over a half a million snowmobiles will be added to the sport, and with this many people participating, deaths must be expected. This is why it is very important for all snowmobilers to have first aid knowledge and skills that in an emergency may save a life or prevent serious complications as well as minimize pain and suffering.

General Instructions

If a medical emergency arises you must remember that the assistance given is only temporary. It is also very important that you know what you are doing, and if you don't, you are better off waiting for someone who does. Listed below are general directions that should be followed and will remain the same no matter what the problem is.

1. Remain calm and keep others calm.
2. Analyze your situation and make a decision as to your capability of handling it by yourself with the skill and information you possess. It is better to do nothing than to do something wrong that might cause further damage or death.
3. Analyze quickly the circumstances of the problem and the availability of help.
4. Make a decision to act or go for help yourself. If you

decide to act send someone else for help. Make arrangements where you will meet if you have to move the victim off the snowmobile trail.

5. If you have decided to take action, follow these general steps.

a. Keep the injured person lying down until you find out what the problem is.

b. Check first for severe hemorrhage. The injured person may assist you by telling you where there is pain. Winter clothing may not be soaked through with blood so you might have to loosen it carefully. Do not move the victim if possible. You must stop severe bleeding first or it may be fatal.

c. After you have controlled bleeding, check respiration. In very cold weather this can easily be done by looking for breath in the cold air. If the person is not breathing, apply mouth to mouth resuscitation as described by the American Red Cross. If necessary also administer external heart massage.

d. Next, check for fractures and splint where necessary.

e. If bleeding, respiration, and broken bones are not threats to the victim you must now treat for shock. Remember that there must be something under the person as well as over him to conserve body heat (see section on shock).

f. If the person is unconscious or semiconscious, turn the head to the side to avoid choking if he should happen to vomit. When he turns very white the unconsciousness is in most cases due to shock. However, if he is blue, there may be an obstruction in the throat that must be cleared immediately.

g. Note the general appearance and listen carefully to

complaints. Check respiration and pulse while checking for the obvious injuries. It is important to be sure you have at least tried to locate them all. If necessary, cut away rather than remove clothing on the extremities. You can always wrap the clothing around the arm or leg after you have administered first aid. In below-freezing weather expose skin only if absolutely necessary.

h. In most cases you will have to give aid and then prepare to transport the injured person to the closest road that can be reached by car or ambulance. If the injury has occurred on a road, move the person only if absolutely necessary. You may park snowmobiles in a way so traffic will have to go around him. Have someone direct traffic until authorities arrive.

i. Do not give the injured liquids, including alcoholic beverages. *Never* give liquids to an unconscious person.

j. Keep people not involved in the first aid procedure away.

k. Keep the injured person comfortable and calm and don't let him see his injury if possible.

l. Give the assistance rapidly but carefully.

m. Do not move the person unnecessarily, and when moving do it with extreme caution following the rules of proper transportation.

n. Do not allow the injured person to get up or move until you are absolutely sure in your own mind that he is not seriously injured.

o. It is advisable to have all injuries checked by a physician as a problem may develop later on—too late for any help.

Special Considerations

There are many winter conditions that affect the administration of first aid in cold climates, and the snowmobiler must become familiar with them. Because of certain conditions of weather, there are times when long snowmobile excursions should be avoided. Even if you feel you have appropriate clothing, weather conditions may become such that the clothing is insufficient to maintain adequate body warmth. If a body part becomes too cold it may become damaged (see section on frostbite). Sitting on a snowmobile allows for very little physical exertion that is necessary to keep blood circulation adequate for the external temperature. When circulation is impaired, the chance of injury also becomes greater. While snowmobiling, you must first be sure that you are dressed for conditions, and second, when snowmobiling becomes greatly uncomfortable because of the cold, the trip should be terminated. Remember too that the thermal temperature is not the true temperature (see wind chill chart), and on the majority of days the actual temperature is a great deal lower than recorded. Add to this inactivity and increased wind chill from a moving vehicle and one will find a sufficient reason for being sensible about snowmobiling.

Years ago it was believed that when the body became cold, rubbing it would stimulate circulation. While snowmobiling if you find you are so cold that you would like to rub your skin, this is an indication your body is becoming too cold. It is important for older people, especially those with circulatory problems, not to expose themselves to cold weather for very long periods of time. Poor circulation makes a person less resistant to cold. It might be wise for these people to carry with them a thermos of hot coffee or tea. It is erroneous to think that alcoholic beverages will be helpful. For your own safety and the safety of others do not mix alcohol and snowmobiles.

If an injury were to occur on a trail where it becomes necessary to expose skin, it is wise to complete all first aid as soon as possible. Remember with all injuries there is some degree of traumatic shock and it is important to conserve body heat to avoid complications. This cannot be done if the injured area is exposed directly to the elements for a long period of time. Some new ideas on exposing bleeding parts to cold in order to lower temperature and impair circulation has been debated, and in most cases this procedure is not recommended for the type of accident that a snowmobiler might have. Great harm and greater damage may be the result of exposure. When applying first aid on the trail you must treat the injury and then protect it from the weather by covering the dressed area with an adequate amount of clothing.

If the trip to the nearest medical facility will involve a great deal of time and there is a bleeding wound involved, it is wise to check the wound often because if blood is allowed to soak into clothing fabrics, the insulating effect is greatly reduced. Also bleeding control techniques may have to be used again due to the movement involved in snowmobile transportation. It is always a good idea to check the injured person often while transporting him. If you have allowed him to take a position on the snowmobile behind you, it might be wise to secure him to you as it would be difficult for you to prevent him from falling off. Keep talking to him.

A new concept in treating burns is the application of cold to the area. However, if the burns are severe, the first aider must be very careful about administering this method. If shock is great, circulation will be greatly impaired, and it must be carefully considered how much the total body temperature will be lowered when treating a large burned area.

Another common problem on the snowmobile trail is snow blindness (see section on snow blindness). Therefore, to prevent this problem from occurring it is wise to wear goggles or sun glasses on bright days when the sun is glaring off ice and snow. Even dull days can produce snow blindness so it is better to take this precaution and wear the glasses.

One last consideration on the snowmobile trail is overexposure, which may result in freezing. To avoid this problem, terminate snowmobile trips when symptoms first appear. If this is not possible you must keep the person physically moving to keep circulation sufficient in the extremities. It might be wise to stop and have the person walk with assistance behind the snowmobile. If there is freezing of a foot or leg it is very important not to use this part until it can be rethawed by proper methods. When freezing occurs, this person will most likely need to be transported by any of the litter methods discussed under transportation.

Transportation

Transporting a snowmobile accident victim is a very serious and important aspect of first aid that cannot be considered lightly. Most injuries will probably occur in areas that are inaccessible for most mechanized vehicles, placing the responsibility for getting the injured person to medical help on the person administering the first aid. In most cases improper or careless transportation is much more important than speedy transportation.

General Transportation Procedure

After first aid has been given and it is decided that the injured person must be moved, the type of transportation needed in relation to the injury must be considered. In most cases if the person has a minor injury or one that permits sitting, he can ride the snowmobile without creating further damage. However, the snowmobile still must be driven slowly and carefully. If the injury requires the person to be lying down, the only way he can be moved is by a pulled litter. The snowmobile sled or seat is not long enough to allow someone to lie down. This is the reason why it is important to have a tarpaulin along, as it can be tied between two eight-foot tree limbs to make a litter. Another method would be to afix the tarpaulin litter to a sled as long as no part of the body would touch points where the litter rested. An ambulance litter can't track behind a snowmobile because of the collapsible wheels, but it may be placed on a cargo sled. If a toboggan is available this will transport an injured person nicely as long as it is not pulled very fast. If a sleeping bag is available, maintaining body warmth will be no problem.

If the person is seriously ill, or has head, back, neck or leg injuries, the only way he can be transported is on a litter. If the accident has occurred on a road it is wise not to move the person but just wait for an ambulance to arrive while giving first aid.

Back injuries need special care. Because of the position of the body while riding a snowmobile, the chance of having a back injury is greater. If the injured person is believed to have a broken back he must be moved in a face-down position. If it is believed to be a fractured pelvis, the victim must be transported in a face-up position. In moving a person with a fracture, the fracture must first be splinted and supported during all movement. In building a litter for back injuries, it is important that the area supporting the back be stiff. If this is necessary, several eight-foot branches should be used with twigs and branches placed crosswise and covered with as much material as possible to make this stiff.

There may be several incidents where getting to proper medical facilities is imperative, and spending time to build a litter may not be in the best interest of the injured person. If he can assume a sitting position then he should be strapped to the snowmobile driver and taken directly to medical facilities.

First Aid Kits

The best first aid kits are commercial products whose contents have been recommended by physicians and professional medical organizations. If purchasing a kit is not feasible, then most of the following items may be obtained to meet the majority of emergencies. Most commercial first aid kits contain only enough material to handle a single emergency, therefore after each use, the kit should be replenished. Contents will be clearly marked, but care must be taken to read each label carefully. Most manufacturers have refill kits that may be purchased where you obtained the original kit.

If you make your own kit, keep the following information in mind.

1. Pack items so they will not be crushed or broken.
2. All contents must be shatterproof.
3. Make the kit as compact as possible so it may be kept permanently on the snowmobile.
4. Wrap items so that unused portions will not become contaminated with handling.
5. Arrange the kit so items may be found quickly.

The following list covers most items which will be needed in any one emergency:

  3 one-inch roller bandages
  2 two-inch roller bandages
  1 package two-inch sterile gauze pads
  1 one-half ounce absorbent cotton balls
  2 one-inch adhesive tape rolls
  6 sterile eye pads
  1 triangular bandage
  1 tourniquet
  1 liquid antiseptic
  1 bar antiseptic soap or liquid soap
  1 box ammonia inhalants
  1 tube of burn ointment
10 cotton swabs
  2 wood splints
  1 scissors
  1 tweezers
  2 plastic cups
  1 box plastic food wrap
  1 box plastic bags
  1 elastic wrap bandage
  1 package three-inch sterile gauze pads
  2 packages adhesive bandages

The following are problems that might occur on a snowmobile trail. Each subject is discussed in relation to causes and special considerations, identification, and treatment.

Animal Bites

Special Considerations

All animal bites produce a puncture wound that in many cases is serious. Bites by mammals both domestic and wild also carry the danger of rabies. If there is any doubt about the animal, it should be confined or killed in order to be examined. If the animal cannot be obtained for examination, the bitten person must undergo a series of painful shots as there is no cure for rabies. Do not harass or molest wild life on the snowmobile trail. Avoid teasing pets and never allow children to play roughly with any animal.

Treatment

If there is a problem of getting medical help immediately, clean the wound with soap and water. The bitten person must be seen by a physician within 24 hours for the Pasteur treatment against rabies.

Back Injury

Causes and Special Considerations

The position of the body on the snowmobile tends to increase the possible danger of back injuries. Anytime the snowmobile leaves the ground the force of the return impact places great pressure on the bones, muscles, and ligaments of the back. Snowmobiles have a problem of getting stuck in snowbanks once in a while and back injuries are common for people who are unaccustomed to lifting such heavy weights. This type of back injury can be greatly reduced if the proper lifting position is used to free immobilized snowmobiles. If the back is kept erect, with feet firmly planted, the strong large muscles of the legs and thighs can assist in the lift, which distributes the weight more evenly along the vertebral column. If a high-speed accident should occur there is a dangerous possibility of also fracturing the bones of the back. If this happens, proper transportation of the injured is extremely important in order to prevent further damage to the spinal cord, which runs through the vertebral column.

Identification

In back strain there is severe pain that increases with movement. The symptoms will increase in intensity for several hours after the injury. The strain generally is accompanied by severe muscle spasms that may bolt a person to a position. No first aider should make a diagnosis of back strain, because the symptoms of other injuries such as low back sprain, herniated intervertebral disc, and other orthopedic problems produce similar symptoms. However, the first aid for most of these problems is quite similar. With a broken back there may or may not be unconsciousness. There may be severe pain along the spinal column with a particular pain in one spot, or deformity of the back. Sometimes there is an inability to move the feet or toes. Even though this paralysis may not be permanent, improper movement may make it so.

Treatment

First consider a broken back. If the symptoms indicate there is a possibility, it is better not to move the victim at all until the aid of a number of people trained to handle such injuries arrives. If all other possibilities are not feasible, and it is the last resort to move the injured person, he must be moved in a face-down position on something rigid. It is important to splint the back before any movement is made. This can best be done by wrapping tree limbs to the body so they may be used to lift the person onto the litter. If a broken back has been ruled out the individual must be placed in a position in which there is no back pain. On the snowmobile trail it may be necessary to build a litter if the injured person finds it impossible to sit on the snowmobile. Moist heat application is a basic treatment but impossible on a snowmobile trail. It may ease the pain if a tight strap is affixed to the back area around the winter clothing. A triangular bandage held in place by roller bandage may be used to strap the back if the triangular bandage is not large enough to go around the body. The injured person should be seen by a physician for an accurate diagnosis.

Bleeding Control

Causes and Special Considerations

Accidents that cause hemorrhage (bleeding) can be of various types, but they fall into two major classes: external, called arterial from arteries, and venous, which comes from veins; and internal, which is bleeding within the body. Most external bleeding will be obvious and can be cared for by standard methods. Internal bleeding also gives its characteristic symptoms and can be handled according to standard first aid procedures regardless of the temperature or weather conditions.

Identification

With arterial bleeding, the blood color will be bright red, will spurt from the wound, and is usually profuse. In venous bleeding, the blood color will be dark-red and will ooze from the wound. It is easier to control venous bleeding than arterial bleeding. In any case, blood loss of over two and a half quarts is usually fatal, especially when the loss is within a short period of time. Internal bleeding within the chest, abdomen, or pelvic cavities is usually brought about by a tremendous force that tears or ruptures internal organs or blood vessels. After an injury, if a person goes into a state of shock, which is characterized by a pale facial color, rapid irregular pulse, dizziness, faintness, cold clammy skin, dilated pupils, shallow irregular breathing, and thirst, and if he has accompanying internal pain or rectal, oral, or urinary bleeding, the possibility of internal bleeding must be suspected.

Treatment

Direct pressure on the bleeding vessel is the most effective treatment for external bleeding. If possible a sterile dressing should be used when applying the direct finger pressure. It takes several minutes for blood clots to form. In most cases, speed is of greatest importance. Arterial bleeding usually can be controlled by direct pressure. However, it may be an added advantage to use the pressure point method of control in which the artery is pressed at a point between the wound and the heart where the artery crosses bones. If all other methods fail, a tourniquet may be used, but this must be the last resort and must never be held in place for longer than 15 to 20 minutes. A tourniquet is a flat-surfaced material that will not cut the skin and is tightened by twisting the material a few inches

above a wound. It must be remembered that the tourniquet also cuts off the blood supply to healthy tissues. These
tissues cannot live without their blood nourishment, therefore it is important that the tourniquet is loosened to allow
some blood to reach these tissues. Another problem with
tourniquets is that of the formation of blood clots. Some
clots that are formed at the injury site are dislodged when
the tourniquet is ' osened. The first aider must consider
this problem and if possible get the victim to medical help
within the 15 to 2. minute time period. If a tourniquet
is made, the time of its application must be noted and it
should be tightened only enough to control the bleeding.
Remember a tourniquet should be used only for the control of life-threatening bleeding that does not respond to
direct or pressure point bleeding control. Shock is also
very great in serious bleeding (see section on shock control) .

A special problem—nosebleed—can occur on the snowmobile trail '   lt of a head injury or because of the
dry, cold w   one does occur and sterile gauze or
cotton is available, place a small piece in the nostril that
is bleeding. It also helps to place a small bit under the lip
between the gums while firmly pressing the nostrils together. Cold snow on the nose or back of the neck may
help. Remove the gauze or cotton very gently after 5 to 10
minutes. A large clot will usually come with the removal of
this material, which may cause the nose to bleed again.

Burns

Causes and Special Considerations

Burns on a snowmobile trail will occur from a burned
hand from touching a hot snowmobile part to severe burns

from a forest fire. Basically, burns are quite painful unless they are so deep that they injure the nerves. Burns are divided into three groups: first degree (superficial injury), second degree (deep injury, which extends into the deeper layers of skin and causes a leakage of fluid from the blood), third (severe destruction of skin and underlying tissue that may actually be charred). The seriousness of the burn will determine the treatment.

Identification

First degree burns are characterized by a reddening of the skin, which is very painful. Second degree burns are characterized by reddening and the formation of blisters; pain is usually great, especially if the area is quite large. Third degree burns are full thickness burns and a combination of first and second degree burns. It is very difficult to judge the degree and extent of the burn immediately after the injury has taken place.

Treatment

Avoid traditional butter. If a burn ointment from the first aid kit is available, the area should be covered and a dressing and bandage applied. It may help to put snow and ice into a plastic bag and apply it directly to the area to reduce shock. If the burn covers a large area medical assistance should be secured as soon as possible.

Drowning and Resuscitation

Causes and Special Considerations

The only chance for the snowmobiler to become involved in a water accident is when the snowmobile breaks through the ice. It is recommended that snowmobiles should not travel on ice less than nine inches deep, and this may be checked by chopping a hole in the ice. When a person has lost consciousness and is not breathing as a result of a water mishap, speed in getting him breathing again is very important.

Identification and Treatment

As the result of a water accident, a person can be unconscious and not breathing. He will appear blue in color. Water in the mouth may be removed by pressing the stomach. Mouth-to-mouth resuscitation must be started immediately and continued for at least one hour or until help arrives. If no pulse is felt, external heart massage is also recommended. Treat for shock.

Electrical Shock—High-voltage Type

Causes and Special Considerations

If for some reason a snowmobiler has come in contact with a high-voltage wire it is very important that he is removed from the contact as soon as possible. It is also important to understand the peril the rescuer is under if an attempt is made to remove the victim. Electrical current is affected by weather conditions (snow and ice) and also has the ability to jump from the power line to the nearest ground (the rescuer). In attempting a rescue do not expose yourself to the power line or the contact. Do not attempt to remove the person from the wire but try to remove the wire from the person. Contact with the wire should be made only by a non-conducting substance such as rubber or dry paper. In all cases the material must be completely dry. On snow or ice breaking contact is difficult—if not impossible—as the rescuer must also be standing on a dry non-conductive material. Prolonged exposure to high-voltage current will cause death.

Identification

Obvious contact with a wire. Sometimes flashes can be seen leaping from the bare wire. The victim will be unconscious with a weak or absent pulse. Breathing will have ceased and there will be contact burns.

Treatment

Mouth-to-mouth resuscitation with external heart massage. Always treat for traumatic shock.

Eye Injuries

Causes and Special Considerations

While snowmobiling, the head often becomes the target of injuries. Often it is held above the windshield, and this is when most eye injuries occur. Sometimes a small piece of tree bark or dirt gets caught in the eye and in most cases can be wiped out with a small piece of moist sterile gauze. However, the eye is a very delicate organ and can easily be injured. It is recommended that when the eye is injured it should just be patched until proper medical help can be obtained. If there are no symptoms of head injuries, the victim may be transported by snowmobile.

Identification

There is usually pain in the eye and a feeling that there is something in it.

Treatment

If the irritation cannot be removed easily with a damp cloth the eye should be covered with gauze and affixed with tape.

Fainting and Unconsciousness

Causes and Special Considerations

If a person faints or becomes unconscious on the snow-mobile trail there may be a variety of causes. When examining an unconscious person always check for bleeding and stoppage of breathing. After that, check for head injuries by examining the size of the pupils. Never give any liquids to an unconscious person.

Treatment

Loosen all tight clothing. If there is no bleeding and the face is blue, the possibility of an obstruction in the throat must be considered. In the case of the tongue dropping back to block the air passageway, you may force the jaw open by pressing at the joint of the jaw and pulling the tongue forward. If there are other obstructions they must be removed before any mouth-to-mouth resuscitation is possible. If simple fainting is suspected, have the person lie down with the knees bent or sit with the head between the knees. Snow on the back of the neck may also help. All forms of unconsciousness constitute a medical emergency and require immediate medical help. If vomiting occurs keep the head in a position so the person will not inhale any material. If convulsions begin, place a stick in the mouth to prevent injury to the tongue, teeth, or jaws. Always treat for shock.

Fractures

Causes and Special Considerations

Fractures occur when a bone has come in contact with a specific force that causes the bone to crack or completely break. A simple fracture is a break that does not penetrate the skin, while a compound fracture causes a wound to occur where the bone has penetrated the skin. Bones not only are broken by blows but also by muscles being torn from their moorings. The majority of fractures that occur while snowmobiling are caused by direct falls from the moving vehicle. If the fracture could be considered minor (finger or toe) the injured person could be transported by riding on the snowmobile. If the break concerns an arm or leg he may need to be transported by litter.

Identification

A fall or blow that causes pain, swelling, and the inability to move the portion of the body below the fracture site. If the fracture is compounded, the bone will be protruding from a wound that is bleeding.

Treatment

The fracture site must be made immovable, both above and below the point of breakage. If there is an open wound the bleeding must be stopped by direct pressure, or if this is impossible, the other methods of hemorrhage control. Never attempt to set the fracture. Treat for shock, if symptoms appear.

Fracture	Identification	Treatment and transportation
Head	Person may or may not be unconscious. Blood may come from ears, nose, or mouth. Pupils may be unequal.	Keep on back. Treat for shock. Do not allow to get up, and transport flat on back with head immobilized.
Pelvis	Pain in the pelvic area. Shock is severe. Inability to lift heal while on the back.	Move the injured only while lying on the back. Keep the knees and ankles together. The whole body should be strapped to the litter.

Arm	Pain, tenderness, swelling in the arm with an inability to move fingers.	Splint and immobilize above and below the break. Transport by litter or snowmobile.
Leg	Severe pain, tenderness, and swelling in the area of the break. Fracture of the upper leg is more serious in most cases. The foot may be turned outward.	Immobilize and splint from the underarm to the foot and transport only by litter.
Rib	Severe pain in rib area and on inspiration of air. Most cases the bones are just cracked; however a severe break may puncture a lung bringing up bright red blood from the mouth.	Do not expose chest to elements. Use triangular bandage to support the area. If the lung is believed to be punctured, do not bandage. Transport by litter to avoid further damage.
Finger	Pain, tenderness, and swelling with an enlargement of the knuckle.	Splint finger in a straight position and transport by snowmobile.
Wrist	Wrist deformity, pain, tenderness, and swelling.	Immobilize whole hand and transport by snowmobile.
Ankle	Pain, swelling, tenderness, and discoloration on the top or side of the foot.	Support the ankle with a triangular or elastic bandage. Return foot to boot if possible. Even though you might think the ankle is only sprained it should be seen by a doctor for an accurate diagnosis. Transport by snowmobile.
Kneecap	Pain, tenderness and swelling at the knee joint with an inability to strengthen the leg. Sometimes bone fragments may be felt in the knee area.	Splint from thigh to foot and transport on a litter.

Frostbite and Overexposure

Causes and Special Considerations

Sometimes while enjoying snowmobiling you may fail to realize how cold the areas of your body that are susceptible to frostbite are. As a result, hands, feet, ears, and nose may become frozen. If the frozen portion is not rewarmed in a reasonable period of time, the danger of gangrene is great, and may result in the loss of a part or a portion of a part. In overexposure, the whole body is affected, causing the person to become sluggish and very drowsy, perhaps to a point of unconsciousness. Frostbite tends to occur when there is a high wind.

Identification

Overexposure: numbness that is associated with a difficulty in moving. There is sluggishness, visual difficulties, and possible unconsciousness.

Frostbite: discolored skin (yellow or white), coldness, and a tingling feeling. There is intense pain or no pain at all. When thawing the frozen part out, there will be severe pain.

Treatment

Treat for shock and if there is no breathing give mouth-to-mouth resuscitation. Do not attempt to rewarm frostbitten parts until the person is indoors and off the snowmobile trail. When the victim is brought in from the cold weather, if conscious he should be given warm drinks such as coffee or tea. He should be wrapped in a blanket to allow warming to take place. If frostbite accompanies the overexposure, the thawing process should be gradual. Never rub the frostbitten area or further damage may take place. If blisters have been formed, apply a dry dressing and encourage moving the frostbitten part to stimulate circulation.

Gunshot Wound

Causes and Special Considerations

Gunshot wounds that might be received during hunting season are treated like a puncture wound (see wounds). There is a danger of a bone fracture, which also must be considered when treating the wound. Because puncture wounds generally do not bleed freely and are usually difficult to clean, the danger of infection is great. If the wound has torn through skin and tissue, bleeding may also be present. There is also great danger of life threatening internal bleeding caused by severing an internal organ or blood vessel.

Identification

There is a perforation in the skin that is red or blue in color. There may be profuse bleeding or hardly any at all. If the shotgun blast was at close range there may be blue-black powder burns around the wound. The victim may or may not be unconscious. Shock is great in relation to the seriousness of the wound.

Treatment

Although a great loss of blood may be a dangerous thing, there should be some bleeding from the wound to flush out infectious germs. Bleeding may be encouraged by pressing the area around the wound with a sterile piece of gauze. In excessive bleeding, direct pressure in most cases will control it. If this method fails, the other methods of hemorrhage control may be used (see bleeding control). On the trail about the only thing to do is control bleeding, splint fractures, treat for shock, and transport the injured person to medical facilities as quickly as possible. If it will be some time before medical help can be obtained, foreign material or pellets can be washed from the wound by pouring cooled boiled water on the wound. If a clean tweezers is available from a first aid kit, pellets may be removed if not deep. If signs of infection are present, wet, hot compresses will help. After cleaning the wound, apply a sterile dressing and bandage. If pellets or bullets are deep they should not be removed as greater damage may occur.

Head Injuries

Causes and Special Considerations

Head injuries from a snowmobile accident usually take the form of a concussion or skull fracture. If a head injury occurs do not be concerned which it is, as the treatment on the snowmobile trail is the same. A concussion is a bruise on the brain that is accompanied by an immediate period of unconsciousness of various duration. Skull fracture will have similar symptoms.

Identification

The presence of a cut or bump that may be quite large due to swelling by fluid or blood. The victim may be dazed or completely unconscious. With a fracture there may be bleeding from the nose, mouth, ears, or all three. The pulse may be weak but rapid. The pupils of the eyes may be unequal and there may be a partial paralysis of a body part.

Treatment

The victim must be kept lying down. Treat for shock and move him only by litter. If there is bleeding from the ears, nose, or mouth, keep the head turned to one side. If there is a wound, apply a dressing if available. Control any excessive bleeding by methods established under bleeding control.

Shock

Causes and Special Considerations

It must be remembered that with all trauma there is some degree of shock, which is usually in proportion to the severity of the injury. Shock is caused by a drop in the pressure of the blood as the body responds to the stress it is withstanding. Any fluid loss will greatly increase the shock.

Identification

The injured person will become quite pale. He may lose consciousness. The skin becomes cold and wet with perspiration as the body temperature drops. Pupils become dilated and breathing becomes shallow and irregular. If the person is still conscious he will be dizzy or may faint. There may be a feeling of great thirst, nausea, and vomiting. The person may seem to be in a daze or disoriented from his environment.

Treatment

Remember that shock accompanied by an injury, either physical or emotional, must first be treated as directed. Always keep the person quiet and in a position that has been designated for his particular problem. If possible, unless there is obvious head injury, the shock position where the feet are elevated while the victim is lying down is highly recommended. It is important to keep the victim warm, and on the snowmobile trail this means something under as well as over the person. Shock is increased with pain. Try to administer first aid to the injury, which will alleviate considerable pain. If conscious and thirsty, liquids may be given when available. Sugar or salt seems to help and can be given in snow. Alcoholic beverages should never be given.

Sprain and Strain

Causes and Special Considerations

Strains are injuries to muscles or tendons that are stretched or ruptured causing a swelling of surrounding tissues. Sprains are injuries to muscles and ligaments around joints. Both are usually caused by a severe twisting and both damage surrounding tissue. The recommended treatment is to put the injured part to rest and apply cold to the area within a 12-hour period to control swelling. Some medical people however prefer to keep the injured joint active even though there is considerable pain. This apparently minimizes swelling and hemorrhage of the small blood vessels in the injured area and allows for a faster recovery. The only problem is that there is no positive way of determining whether the injury is a sprain or a bone fracture in which further activity could result in more serious damage. On the snowmobile trail it might be wise to be conservative.

Treatment

Sprain: rest, elevate when possible, and apply cold compresses. Snow and ice in a plastic bag may help. Im-

mobilize the area by strapping with the triangular bandage or elastic bandage. If it is an ankle, return the foot to the snowmobile boot for added protection.
Strain: rest and allow the person to assume a position in which there is little pain for the injured part. Massage to the injured area may help but it would be better not to expose the injury to the winter elements.

Snow Blindness

Causes and Special Considerations

It is always wise to use sun glasses while snowmobiling to decrease the glare off the snow.

Identification

If glasses have not been used and the day is bright, the eyes may begin to feel gritty and painful and then turn red. Even a dull day may cause these same symptoms, but they will occur more rapidly in bright sunlight. There is an urge to rub the eyes and bright objects cause pain when stared at.

Treatment

The eyes should be covered (at least one at a time if it is necessary to drive the snowmobile) and cold compacts applied. The person must not be out in sun glare until the pain and redness have gone away. Mineral oil helps to eliminate the gritty feeling.

Wounds

Causes and Special Considerations

A wound is a breaking of the skin. Bleeding is the first consideration. When bleeding is minimal it should be considered good, as it washes germs and contaminated material from the wound. However, loss of a great deal of blood is a life-threatening problem. There are two important considerations in the problem of wounds. First, the amount of bleeding, and second, the danger of infection. If a wound occurs on the snowmobile trail it is very important to have sterile first aid equipment available to treat it. Once the bleeding has been controlled, the danger of infection must be considered. If the wound is severe with a great deal of bleeding the victim must be seen by a physician as soon as possible.

Identification

Puncture: This wound appears as a small hole in the skin usually without much loss of blood.

Contusion: A common bruise that appears black and blue without skin breakage.

Abrasion: A scraping of the skin with little bleeding.

Avolution: A wound where tissue has been torn from the body.

Laceration: A tearing of tissue accompanied by severe bruising.

Incised: A clean surgical type cut, usually deep with free flowing blood.

Treatment

First the bleeding must be stopped by direct pressure. If this does not stop the bleeding then the pressure point procedure or a tourniquet must be used. After bleeding has been controlled, the area should be washed with soap and water. A sterile dressing should be applied and affixed by bandage or tape. If the wound is severe the edges can be drawn together by tape called a butterfly bandage. Severe wounds must be seen by a physician in case they must be sutured. Always treat for shock.

Appendix

Snowmobile and Other Vehicle Manufacturers

Members of the International Snowmobile
Industry Association

AMF/York, Whiteford Road, York, Pennsylvania 17402

Arctic Enterprises, Inc., PO Box 167, Thief River Falls, Minnesota 56701

Ariens Company, 655 West Ryan Street, Brillion, Wisconsin 54110

Boa-Ski, Div. Giffen Ind., PO Box 7, LaGuadeloupe, Cte. Frontenac, Quebec, Canada

Boatel Co., Inc., Div. Telecheck International, 24 North Walnut St., Mora, Minnesota 55051

Bolens Division, FMC Corp., 215 S. Park St., Port Washington, Wisconsin 53074

Bombardier, Ltd., Valcourt, Quebec, Canada

Chaparral Industries, Div. FTS Corp., 5995 N. Washington St,. Denver, Colorado 80216

Eskimo Snowmobile Inc., Div. Agritek, Inc., 91 Hymus Blvd., Pointe Claire, Canada

Evinrude Motors, Division OMC, 4143 N. 27th Street, Milwaukee, Wisconsin 53545

Featherweight Corporation, Subs. Bangor Punta, 101 Louvain St., Montreal, Canada

Fox Corporation, 1111 W. Racine St., Janesville, Wisconsin 53545

Industries Bouchard, Inc., Subs. Giffen Industries, LaPoca-
tiere, Quebec, Canada

Johnson Motors, Div. OMC, 200 Pershing Rd., Waukegan,
Illinois 60085

Lionel Enterprises, Inc., Subs Giffen Ind., 725 St. Henri,
Princeville, Quebec

Massey-Ferguson, Inc., 1901 Bell Ave., Des Moines, Iowa 50322

Outboard Marine Corp., 100 Pershing Rd., Waukegan, Illinois
60085

Outboard Marine Corp. of Canada, Peterborough, Ontario,
Canada

Polaris Industries, Inc. Div. Textron, Roseau, Minnesota 56751

Polaris Industries of Canada, Ltd., Div. Textron, Beausejour,
Manitoba, Canada

Rupp Manufacturing, Inc., 1785 Airport Rd., Mansfield, Ohio
55903

Scorpion, Inc., Div. Fuqua, Inc., PO Box 300, Crosby, Minnesota 56441

Skiroule, Ltee Route 13, Wickham, Cte. Drummond, Quebec,
Canada (Div. Coleman Co.)

Sno-Jet, Inc., Division Glastron Boat, Thetford-Mines, Quebec,
Canada

A. B. Westerasmaskiner, 740-41 Morgongava, Sweden

Wheel Horse Products, Inc., 515 W. Ireland Rd., South Bend,
Indiana 46614

Yamaha Motor Co., Ltd., 1280 Nakajo, Hamakita City, Shizu-
oka Pre., Japan

Associate Members

ACS Limited, 114 Railside Road, Don Mills, Ontario, Canada

Canadian Curtiss Wright, Ltd., 500 Carlingview Dr., Rexdale,
Ontario, Canada

Curtiss-Wright Corporation, 1 Passaic St., Wood-Ridge, New
Jersey 07075

Dayco Corporation, 333 First Street, Dayton, Ohio 45401

Donaldson Co., Inc., 1400 W. 94th St., Minneapolis, Minnesota 55431

Fichtel & Sachs Aktiengesellschaft, Ernst-Sachs-Strasse 62–872 Schweinfurt/M Bundesrepublik, Deutschland

Kohler Co., Kohler, Wisconsin 53044

Kohler of Canada Ltd., 6390 Northwest Dr., Malton, Ontario, Canada

Rockwell Mfg. Co., 400 North Lexington Avenue, Pittsburgh, Pennsylvania 15208

Rotax-Werk, A. G. Gunskirchen, Austria

Sachs Motors Corp., Ltd., 9615 Cote de Liesse, Dorval 700, Quebec, Canada

Tecumseh Products Co., Grafton, Wisconsin 53024

Tillotson Mfg. Co., 760 Berdan Ave., Toledo, Ohio 43610

Wisconsin Motor Corp., 1910 South 53rd St., Milwaukee, Wisconsin 53246

Germany and Other European Manufacturers

Lohner-Werke, 2, Parzellangasse, Wien 9, Austria

OY Metaxo Ltd., Sahaajankatu 31, Helsinki, Finland

SOK Helsingin Tehtaat, Fleminginkatu 36, Helsinki, Finland

Velsa OY, Kurikka, Finland

Messrs. Alois Kober KG, Maschinenfabrik, PO Box 260, 8870 Guenzburg, Germany

ISO S.P.A. Automotoveicoli 1-20091 Bresso, Milano, Italy

A. B. Westerasmaskiner S-740, 41 Morgongava, Sweden

Ockelbo Industri AB. S-816 oo Ockelbo, Sweden

Monark-Crescent AB. Box 141 S-432 oo Varberg, Sweden

AB Cykelfabriken Fram. Box 3005, S-750 o3 Uppsala, Sweden

Joba AB. S 782 oo Malung, Sweden

Manufacturers Not Members as of February 1970

CMC Corp., Scranton, Pennsylvania (Ski-Jet)

Courarral Co., 1460 Sibley Highway, St. Paul, Minnesota (Sno-Pony)

Frederick Willys, 510 Willow Street, Farmington, Minnesota (Galaxey)

Gilsonbbros Co., PO Box 152, Plymouth, Wisconsin

GO*BYK Ind., Rothsay, Minnesota (Hu-Skee)

Hellstar Corp., 1600 N. Chestnut, Wahoo, Nebraska (Jetstar)

Herter's, Waseca, Minnesota (Huskie-Magnum)

Innovar, Inc., Box 874, Dunnell, Minnesota (Sno-Coupe)

Jac-Trac, PO Box 39, Marshfield, Wisconsin

Jet Dynamics, Inc., PO Box 1131, St. Cloud, Minnesota

Leisure Ind., Inc., 4600 W. 77th St., Suite 227, Minneapolis, Minnesota

Kiekhaeffer-Mercury, 1939 Pioneer Rd., Fond du Lac, Wisconsin (Mercury)

Mallard Coach Corp., PO Box 378, West Bend, Wisconsin (Mallard)

McCormack International Motors, Inc., 17422 Pullman St., Irvine, Wisconsin

Muscat Corp., 50 N.W. 3rd St., Forest Lake, Minnesota (Muscaro)

Poloron Products, Inc., 165 Huguenot St., New Rochelle, N.Y.

Sport Craft, Inc., Mackinaw, Illinois

Sport King, Inc., 28650 Grand River Ave., Farmington, Michigan

Viking Snowmobile, Inc., PO Box 37, Twin Valley, Minnesota

Allcock, Laight and Woods, Bramalea, Ontario, Canada (Arlberg)

Allied Farm Equipment Co., 124 Labrosse Ave., Pte. Clari, Quebec

Eagle Tie and Machine Co., London, Ontario, Canada (Sno-Hawk)

Moto-Neige OOPIK-A/S Jean Marie Gagnon, St. Jean, Port Joli, Quebec (Mini)

Moto Mower, Div. Roper Corp. Intersall, Ontario, Canada (Sno-Commander)

Original Equipment Mfg. Ltd., Sudbury, Canada (Sno-Bug)

S. E. Woods Ltd., 450 Kent Drive, Newmarket, Ontario, Canada (Trail Blazer)

ISOCARS Corp., ISO-Spa-Automotoveicoli, Bresso (Milano), Italy

Information Concerning National Parks and Forests

United States

Alaska—Dept. of Economic Development
    Alaska Travel Division
    Pouch E.
    Juneau, Alaska 99801
Colorado—Colorado Visitors' Bureau
    225 W. Colfax
    Denver, Colorado 80202
Idaho—Dept. of Commerce and Development
    108 Capitol Building
    Boise, Idaho 83701
Maine—Director of Vacation Travel
    State House
    Augusta, Maine 04330
Michigan—Dept. of Natural Resources
    Forestry and Parks Divisions
    Lansing, Michigan 48926
Minnesota—Dept. of Economic Development
    57 W. 7th St.
    St. Paul, Minn. 55012
Montana—Chamber of Commerce
    P. O. Box 1730
    Helena, Montana 59601
Nebraska—Game and Parks Commission
    State Capitol
    Lincoln, Nebraska 68509
New Hampshire—Division of Economic Development
    856 State House Annex
    Concord, New Hampshire 03301
New York—Conservation Dept.
    Division of Lands and Forests
    Albany, New York 12226
North Dakota—Director of Travel
    State Highway Dept.
    Bismarck, North Dakota 58501

Pennsylvania—Bureau of Travel Development
402 South Office Bldg.
Harrisburg, Pennsylvania 17120
South Dakota—Travel Director
State of South Dakota
Pierre, South Dakota 57501
Vermont—Development Dept.
Montpelier, Vermont 05602
Wisconsin—Vacation and Travel Service
P. O. Box 450
Madison, Wisconsin 53701
Wyoming—Travel Commission
2320 Capitol Ave.
Cheyenne, Wyoming 82001

Canada

Travel Bureau
Legislative Bldg.
Edmonton, Alberta

Gov. Travel Bureau
Victoria, British Columbia

Bureau of Travel and Publicity
Winnipeg, Manitoba

Travel Bureau
Fredericton, New Brunswick

Tourist Division Office
St. John's, Newfoundland

Bureau of Information
Halifax, Nova Scotia

Travel Bureau
Charlottetown, Prince Edward Island

Tourist Bureau
Quebec City, Quebec

Tourist Bureau
Legislative Building
Regina, Saskatchewan

Department of Lands and Forests
Parliament Building
Toronto, Ontario

Snowmobile and All-Terrain Vehicle Associations

International Snowmobile Industry Association
734 15th Street N.W.
Washington, D. C. 20005

United States Snowmobile Association
101 Snowmobile Drive
Eagle River, Wisconsin 54521

Canadian All-Terrain Vehicle Manufacturers Association
Contact John Fagan
161 Orenda Rd.
Brampton, Ontario
Canada

Canadian Snowmobile Association
38 St. Vincent
Ste. Agathe Des-Monts, Quebec, Canada

American Snowmobile Association
P. O. Box Columbia Heights 4403
Minneapolis, Minnesota 55403

Maine Snowmobile Association
Box 88
East Winthrop, Maine 04343

Maine Snowmobile Association
269 Center Street
Bath, Maine 04530

Vermont Association of Snowmobiles
Box 411
Hardwick, Vermont 05843

USSA Eastern Division
113 Schuyler Street
Boonville, New York 13309

Western Snowmobile Association
610 Idaho Street
Boise, Idaho 83702

Rocky Mountain Snowmobile Association
P. O. Box 323
Frisco, Colorado 80443

American Snowmobile Racing Association
4403 Columbia Height
Minneapolis, Minnesota 55413

Vermont Association of Snow Travelers
Box 839
Montpelier, Vermont 05602

New Hampshire Snowmobile Association
Box 643
Manchester, New Hampshire 03105

Ontario Federation of Snowmobile Clubs
208 Ring Street
Toronto, Canada

North American Snowmobile Association
18 School Street
Concord, New Hampshire 03301

Snowmobile Council of Massachusetts
Route 20
Westfield, Massachusetts 01085

International Snowmobile Association
9 East Harvey Street
Ely, Minnesota 55731

North Central Marine Association
Association Building
2901 Pleasant Ave.
Minneapolis, Minnesota 55408

Adirondack Snowmobile Association
R.F.D.
Lake Pleasant, New York 12108

Michigan Snowmobile Association
229 W. 15th St.
Traverse City, Michigan 49684

Where to Write for Camping Information

ALASKA
Department of Natural
  Resources
Division of Lands
33 D Street
Anchorage, Alaska 99503

U.S. Forest Service
Recreation and Lands Section
Box 1631
Juneau, Alaska 99801

CALIFORNIA
Department of Natural
Resources
Division of Beaches and Parks
Box 2390
Sacramento, California 95814

COLORADO
Colorado Dept. of Public
  Relations
Capitol Building
Denver, Colorado 80203

CONNECTICUT
State Park and Forest
  Commission
Hartford, Connecticut 06115

DELAWARE
State Development Department
Dover, Delaware 19901

IDAHO
Department of Highways
Box 879
Boise, Idaho 83702
State Land Department
State House
Boise, Idaho 83702

ILLINOIS
Department of Conservation
Division of Parks and Memorials
State Office Building
Springfield, Illinois 61106

MAINE
State Park Commission
State House
Augusta, Maine 04330

Department of Economic
Development
and/or
Maine Forest Service
State House
Augusta, Maine 04330

MARYLAND
Department of Forests
and Parks
State Office Building
Annapolis, Maryland 21401

MASSACHUSETTS
Dept. of Natural Resources
Division of Information and
Education
15 Ashburton Place
Boston, Massachusetts 02108

MICHIGAN
Department of Conservation
Division of Parks and
Recreation
Lansing, Michigan 48933

Michigan Tourist Council
Steven T. Mason Building
Lansing, Michigan 48926

MINNESOTA
Department of Conservation
Division of State Parks
301 Centennial Building
658 Cedar Street
St. Paul, Minnesota 55101

MONTANA
Montana Highway Commission
Helena, Montana 59601

NEW HAMPSHIRE
State Planning and Develop-
ment Commission
Concord, New Hampshire 03301

NEW YORK
State Conservation Department
Division of Parks
State Office Building
Albany, New York 12209

OREGON
Parks and Recreation
Division
Oregon State Highway
Department
301 State Highway Building
Salem, Oregon 97308

PENNSYLVANIA
Division of State Parks
Department of Forests and
Waters
Harrisburg, Pennsylvania 17123

VERMONT
Department of Forests
and Parks
Montpelier, Vermont 05602

WASHINGTON
Washington State Parks
and Rec. Comm.
522 South Franklin Street
Olympia, Washington 23452

WISCONSIN
Wisconsin Conservation
Department
Box 450
Madison, Wisconsin 54301

WYOMING
Wyoming Travel Commission
Capitol Building
Cheyenne, Wyoming 82001

List of Things You May Need
for Your Camping Trip

air mattress
air mattress pump
air mattress repair kit
air pillow
aluminum foil
axe, camp
bed linen
blankets
bottle opener
broom
bucket, canvas
campfire grate
can opener
chairs, folding
charcoal
charcoal grill
chicken fryer
cleanser, household
clothes hangers
clothes line
clothes pins
coffeepot
compass
cots, folding
cups and saucers, plastic
cutting board
detergent
dishes, plastic
dishpan, square plastic
duffel bags
electric lantern
electric lantern batteries
fire lighter disks
first-aid kit
flashlights

food bags, plastic
fork, long-handled
frying pans
gasoline can, funnel
griddle, stove-top
ice chest
ice pick
knife, carving
knife, paring
knife, pocket
lantern, gasoline
lantern mantles
laundry bag, net
lighter fluid
matches
measuring cup
mirror, polished steel
mixing bowls, metal or plastic
nails, assorted
napkins, paper
oven, stove-top
picnic jugs
plates, paper
plates, plastic
pliers, cutting
potholders
pots or nesting camp set
pressure cooker
salt and pepper shaker
saw, bow type
serving spoons
sharpening stone
shears or scissors
shovel, short-handled
sleeping bags

spatula or pancake turner
steak broiler, wire
stove, gasoline, 2 or 3 burners
stove stand
tablecloth, plastic
table cutlery or camper sets
table, folding
table ware
tarpaulin
tent

toaster, folding
toilet articles
toilet tissue
towels or paper toweling
vacuum bottles
wash basin, square plastic
water boiler
water can with spigot
water-purifying filter
water-purifying tablets

Insurance Companies

(There are a number of other companies who also provide coverage)

Agricultural Ins. Group
215 Washington St.
Watertown, New York 13602

All-Star Insurance Corp.
3882 N. Teutonia Ave.
Milwaukee, Wisconsin 53206

American Plan Corp.
American Plan Bldg.
Westbury, L.I., New York
  11590

American States Insurance Co.
542 N. Meridian St.
Indianapolis, Indiana 46206

Austin-St. Paul Ins. Co.
84 S. Sixth St.
Minneapolis, Minnesota 55402

Auto-Owners Insurance Co.
303 W. Kalamazoo St.
Lansing, Michigan 48903

Balboa Insurance Co.
818 W. Seventh St.
Los Angeles, California 90017

Celina Ins. Group
Insurance Square
Celina, Ohio 45822

Continental Nat. Am. Group
310 S. Michigan Ave.
Chicago, Illinois 60604

Employers Mutual Casualty
  Co.
210 Seventh St.
Des Moines, Iowa 50303

Federal Underwriters
Box 5269
Madison, Wisconsin 53705

Foremost Ins. Co.
Grand Rapids, Michigan
  48501

Guarantee Nat. Ins. Co.
916 Broadway
Denver, Colorado 80203

Hallmark Ins. Co.
Box 5269
Madison, Wisconsin 53705

Hawkeye-Security Ins. Co.
1017 Walnut St.
Des Moines, Iowa 50307

Home Ins. Co.
59 Maiden Lane
New York, New York 10008

Jamestown Mutual Ins. Co.
110 East Fourth St.
Jamestown, New York 14701

LaSalle National Ins. Co.
221 N. LaSalle St.
Chicago, Illinois 60601

Midwest Mutual Ins. Co.
Seventh and Walnut Sts.
Des Moines, Iowa 50309

National Indemnity Co.
3024 Harney St.
Omaha, Nebraska 68131

Occidental Fire and Casualty
  Co.
200 Fillmore St.
Denver, Colorado 80206

Reserve Ins. Co.
65 E. South Water St.
Chicago, Illinois 60601

Security Ins. Group
1000 Asylum Ave.
Hartford, Connecticut 06115

Shelby Mutual Ins. Co.
19 Mansfield Ave.
Shelby, Ohio 44875

Stonewall Ins. Co.
2115 Seventh Ave.
Birmingham, Alabama 35203

Sutton Mutual Ins. Co.
Box 810
Rochester, New Hampshire
  03867

Transamerica Insurance
  Group
Occidental Center
Box 54256
Los Angeles, California 90054

United National Ins. Co.
220 S. 16th St.
Philadelphia, Pennsylvania
  19102

Virginia Surety Co., Inc.
200 Fillmore St.
Denver, Colorado 80206

Western Insurance Cos.
14 E. First St.
Fort Scott, Kansas 66701

Wilshire Insurance Co.
5505 Wilshire Blvd.
Los Angeles, California 90036

Wolverine Ins. Co.
70 W. Michigan Ave.
Battle Creek, Michigan 48016

Yosemite Insurance Co.
717 Market St.
San Francisco, California
94103

Snowmobile Trailer Manufacturers

Canada
White Line Mfg.
Box 190
Bavden, Alta., Canada

Connecticut
Bryon Metal Products
Middletown, Connecticut
06457

Florida
Gator Trailers
Box 51 Station G.
Jacksonville, Florida 32206

Idaho
Chukar Mfg.
3800 Chinden Blvd.
Boise, Idaho 83704

Oppel, Inc.
Box 2894
Boise, Idaho 83701

Illinois
John Sterling Co.
Richmond, Illinois 60071

Kentucky
Moore Corp.
Box 1109
Lexington, Kentucky 40501

Michigan
Alloy Marine
4618 Pte. Tremble Rd.
Algonac, Michigan 48001

Maurell Prod. Inc.
2711 S. M 52
Owosso, Michigan 48867

Pardonnet, Mfg.
13263 Merriman Rd.
Livonia, Michigan 48150

R & M Trailer Co.
Ottawa Lake, Michigan 49269

Minnesota
C and F, Ind.
275 E. Marie W.
St. Paul, Minnesota 55118

Lange Mfg.
Pipestone, Minnesota 56164

Pipestone, Mariner Corp.
Box 311
Pipestone, Minnesota 56164

Tag-a Enterprizes
Box 696
Rochester, Minnesota 55901

Herter's Inc.
R.R. 1
Waseca, Minnesota 56093

Nebraska
Snow Corp.
4350 McKinley
Omaha, Nebraska 68112

New Hampshire
Thomson, Corp.
Lancaster, New Hampshire
  03584

New York
Electron Top Mfg.
135-11 Hillside Ave.
Richmond, New York

Semek Mfg.
Townsend Ave.
Johnstown, New York 12095

North Carolina
Cox Trailers
Box 338
Grifton, North Carolina 28530

Ohio
Sterling-Salem Co.
Box 507
Salem, Ohio 44460

Tee Hee Trailer Co.
215 E. Indianola Ave.
Youngstown, Ohio 44507

Pennsylvania
Boyer Industries
12th St.
Erie, Pennsylvania 16501

Texas
Little Dude Co.
Box 4513
Fort Worth, Texas 76106

Nelson-Kykes Co.
4071 Shilling Way
Dallas, Texas 75237

Wisconsin
Balko Inc.
Box 168
Ladysmith, Wisconsin 54848

Calumet Corp.
Box 389
Kankauna, Wisconsin 54130

Fleteway Sales Inc.
138 Front St.
Beaver Dam, Wisconsin 53916

Marion Body Works
Box 26
Marion, Wisconsin 54950

Stark Brothers
Phillips, Wisconsin 54555

All-Terrain Vehicle Manufacturers

AMPHICAT
Mobility Unlimited
44 South Squirrel Rd.
Auburn Heights, Michigan
48057

SKIPPER
ATV Manufacturing Ltd.
81 Lincoln Street
Tillsonburg, Ontario, Canada

TERRA TIGER
Allis-Chalmers
Box 128 L
Lexington, South Carolina
29072

ALL TERRAIN WAGEN
Busse Bros., Inc.
124 N. Columbus St.
Randolph, Wisconsin 53956

PPT (PASSE PAR TOUT)
Valcartier Ind.
P. O. Box 790
Valcartier, Quebec, Canada

MUSCAT
Muscat Corp.
56 E. Broadway
Forest Lake, Minnesota 55025

TRICART
Sperry Rand
New Holland, Pennsylvania
17557

SIERRA TRAIL BOSS
Vesely Co.
2101 N. Lapeer Rd.
Lapeer, Michigan 48446

NANUK
Nanuk, Inc.
91 Hymus Blvd.
Pointe-Claire, 730
Quebec, Canada

WOLVERINE
Wolverine Western
875 W. 16th St.
Newport Beach, California
92660

PAZZAZZ
Air-Lec Industries, Inc.
3300 Commercial Ave.
Madison, Wisconsin 53714

**EXPERIMENTAL MILI-
TARY TERRASTAR**
Lockheed Aircraft Service Co.
Div. Lockheed Aircraft Corp.
Ontario, California

BERRY MINI-T
Berry Corporation
1123 Nevada St.
Long Beach, California 90806

ATTEX
ATV Mfg. Co.
1215 William Flynn
Route 8
Pittsburgh, Pennsylvania
15116

SNOOPY
Coot Ind.
291 World Trade Center
San Francisco, California
94111

CAT-A-GATOR
Mille Lacs Ind., Inc.
Box 8
Ogilvie, Minnesota 56358

CUSHMAN TRACKSTER
Cushman Motors
Outboard Marine Corp.
Lincoln, Nebraska 68503

GIP-SEA
Jasa Mfg. Co., Ltd.
336 Leaside Ave.
Stoney Creek, Ontario, Canada

RIDGE RUNNER
A.S.V.
Ridge Runner, Inc.
1625 Washington St. N.E.
Minneapolis, Minnesota
55413

MF 12 GARDEN TRAC-
TOR
Massey-Ferguson, Inc.
1901 Bell Ave.
Des Moines, Iowa 50315

MULTIMOBILE
Multimobile Corp. Ltd.
3094 Lenworth Dr.
Mississauga, Ontario, Canada

SCRAMBLER
Action-Age, Inc.
18780 Cranwood Parkway
Cleveland, Ohio 44128

JIGER
Breton Versatrek Ltd.
Orenda Rd.
Brampton, Ontario, Canada

MOTO BROUSSE
Atelier Mecanique D'Alma
Ltd.
P. O. Box 204
Alma, P. Q. Canada

RENEGADE
DorLeRey Co.
Havre Highway
Great Falls, Montana

MINI-BRUTE
Feldmann Engineering and
Mfg. Co. Inc.
633-639 Monroe St.
Sheboygan Falls, Wisconsin
53085

Motorcycle Type All-Terrain Vehicles

TRAILMASTER
Yamaha Int. Corp.
Box 54540
Los Angeles, California 90054

FOX MINI-BIKE
Fox Corporation
1111 W. Racine St.
Janesville, Wisconsin 53545

THE ROGUE
Raven Industries, Inc.
Box 1007
Sioux Falls, South Dakota
   57101

EL BURRO
6570 Lake Shore Rd.
Lexington, Michigan 48450

BOONIE-BIKE
Heath Co.
Benton Harbor, Michigan
   49022

TRAIL-BREAKER
Rokon, Inc.
Keene, New Hampshire 03431

SKIWEELS
Ski Wheels, Inc.
448 Park Lane
Barrington, Illinois 60010

Snowmobile Sleigh Manufacturers

Alloy Marine, Inc.
4618 Pte. Tremble Rd.
Algonac, Michigan 48001

Combo Sleds
Cook, Minnesota 55723

Gen. Alum. Prod. Inc.
1023 Reynolds Rd.
Charlotte, Michigan 48813

Griswold Mfg.
Princeton, Minnesota

Les Traineaux de (Riviere-
du-Loup) Inc.
C. P. 271 L
Riviere-du-Loup, Quebec,
   Canada

Mercer Marine Co.
Box 229
Mercer, Wisconsin 54547

Nationwide Industries, Inc.
468 So. Lake St.
Forest Lake, Minnesota 55025

Nick and Sons, Inc.
408 W. Somo Ave.
Tomahawk, Wisconsin 54487

Rademacher Industries, Inc.
S.E. 13th St.
Brainerd, Minnesota 56401

Simoneau Fiberglass, Inc.
139 Rue Principale Ouest
Lyster, Quebec, Canada

Stanley Iron Works
101 W. 79th St.
Bloomington, Minnesota
55420

Sylvan Industries, Inc.
Box 236 W. Elm St.
Millersburg, Indiana 46543

Douglas A. Taylor Co., Inc.
2019 Hudson Ave.
Rochester, New York 14617

Torpedo, Ltd.
3677 Rue Levis
P. O. Box 1395
Lac Megantic, Quebec, Canada

Victor-Lynn Corp.
Chestnut Hill Rd.
Rochester, New Hampshire
03867

Voyager Products, Inc.
1651 E. Brand Blvd.
Detroit, Michigan 48211

Withington Mfg., Inc.
West Minot, Maine 04288

A. W. Allen and Sons, Ltd.
Middleton, Nova Scotia

Cosom Corporation
6030 Wayzata Blvd.
Minneapolis, Minnesota
55416

Fiberez of Canada, Ltd.
P. O. Box 1057
Cornwall, Ontario, Canada

Jim's Sales and Service
Box 168
Gilbert, Minnesota 55741

Maki Sled
Tower, Minnesota 55790

Maurell Products
2711 S. M52
Owosso, Michigan 48867

Pipestone-Mariner Corp.
Box 311
Pipestone, Minnesota 56164

Stark Bros.
Phillips, Wisconsin 54555

Tag-A-Enterprises
Box 45
Mankato, Minnesota 56001

Trayco, Inc.
693 S. Court St.
Lapeer, Michigan 48446

Booklets and Pamphlets

Safe Snowmobile Operation
New York State Conservation
  Dept.
Division of Lands and Forests
Albany, New York 12226

*Arctic Cat Owner's Safety
  Handbook*
Arctic Enterprises, Inc.
Thief River Falls, Minnesota
  56701

*The Snowmobile: What
Makes it Go, What Makes
it Grow*
Bombardier Ltd.
Valcourt, Quebec, Canada

Fun Guide to Snowmobiling
Johnson Motors
Waukegan, Illinois 60085

Snow Cruising Handbook
Evinrude Motors
4143 N. 27th St.   (15¢)
Milwaukee, Wisconsin 53216

*Play Safe For More Winter
Fun*
Bombardier, Ltd.
Valcourt, Quebec, Canada

Wisconsin Snowmobile Map
Evinrude Motors
4143 N. 27th St.
Milwaukee, Wisconsin 53216

Polaris Safety Brochure
Polaris
1400 Park Ave.
Minneapolis, Minnesota
54404

Polaris Trail Guides
1400 Park Ave.
Minneapolis, Minnesota
55404

Eastern Snowmobiler
Boonville, New York 13309

U.S. Dept. of Agriculture
Washington, D. C.
"National Forest Vacations"
"Wilderness"
"Camping"

Superintendent of Documents
U.S. Government Printing
Office
Washington, D. C.
"Checklist National Park
Service"

Proceedings of the International Snowmobile Confer-
ence
Albany, New York

*How to Organize for More
Winter Fun*
Evinrude Motors
4143 North 27th Street
Milwaukee, Wisconsin 53216

Vermont Snowmobile Trails
Vermont Dept. of Forest and
Parks
Montpelier, Vermont 05602

*Instruction on Snowmobile
Safaris*
Heath Rec. Sales Division
Richmond, Michigan 48062

Modern Family Camping
Thermos Co.
Norwich, Connecticut 06360

Snowmobile Trail Guide—
  Michigan
K. E. Sproul
1702 W. Genesee
Saginaw, Michigan 48602

How to Stage a Snowmobile
  Rally
Evinrude Motors
4143 North 27th Street
Milwaukee, Wisconsin 53216

Play Safe with Snowmobiles
Bombardier Ltd.
Valcourt, Quebec, Canada

The Snowmobile Racing
  Primer
Bombardier Ltd.
Valcourt, Quebec, Canada

Snowmobile Drill Teams
Sno-Jet
Box 9668
Austin, Texas 78756

Miscellaneous Information on Snowmobiling

Regional Offices of the National Park Service

REGION 1 900 Lombardy St.
          Richmond, Virginia
REGION 2 307 Federal Office Building
          Omaha, Nebraska
REGION 4 450 Golden Gate Ave.
          San Francisco, California
American Association of Health, Physical Education and
    Recreation
1201 16th Ave. N.W.
Washington, D. C.

Index

213